TALKING PEACE

Talking

A VISION FOR

JIMMY

Peace

THE NEXT GENERATION

FRANKLIN PIERCE
COLLEGE LIBRARY
RINDGE, N.H. 03461

CARTER

Dutton Children's Books | *New York*

Copyright © 1993 by Jimmy Carter
All rights reserved. No part of this publication may be
reproduced or transmitted in any form or by any means,
electronic or mechanical, including photocopy, recording, or
any information storage and retrieval system now known or to
be invented, without permission in writing from the publisher,
except by a reviewer who wishes to quote brief passages in
connection with a review written for inclusion in a magazine,
newspaper, or broadcast.

Library of Congress Cataloging-in-Publication Data

Carter, Jimmy.
Talking peace: a vision for the next generation/by Jimmy Carter.
—1st ed.   p. cm.   Includes index.
Summary: Discusses the various factors involved in peace negotiations and conflict resolution, examining such elements as the
living conditions of citizens in peacetime and wartime and the
effect of international relations on innocent citizens.
ISBN 0-525-44959-0
1. Peace—Juvenile literature.   2. International relations—
Juvenile literature.   3. United States—Foreign relations—
Juvenile literature.   [1. War.   2. Peace.   3. International
relations.   4. United States—Foreign relations.]   I. Title.
JX1953.5.C37 1993
327.1′72—dc20   93-16996   CIP   AC

CURR
JZ
5538
C37
1993

Published in the United States 1993 by
Dutton Children's Books,
a division of Penguin Books USA Inc.
375 Hudson Street, New York, New York 10014

Designed by Sara Reynolds and Chris Welch
Printed in U.S.A.
First edition
10 9 8 7 6 5 4 3

For Annette, Ginger, and Elizabeth

The suggestion that I write *Talking Peace,* to let young people know more about world peace, democracy, and human rights, came from Karen Lotz, an editor at Dutton Children's Books. With the help of Carrie Harmon, communications director for the Carter Center, she outlined the book, drawing from my speeches and writings and on other publications at our center. Susan Palmer, of our Conflict Resolution program, and Peter Wallensteen, of Sweden's Uppsala University, provided information and advice on the world's conflicts. Jay Stevens, an Emory University student intern, helped research inserts and sidebars, and David Bjerklie checked the accuracy of the text. Of special assistance to me were Dr. Steve Hochman, who has worked with me on other books, and Faye Dill, my assistant, who helped to coordinate this combined effort. I am grateful to all of these, and to many others for their contributions.

CONTENTS

INTRODUCTION

As a submarine officer in the U.S. Navy and later as president of the United States, I learned firsthand about the terrible nature of war. This knowledge strengthens my personal commitment to work for the blessings of peace.

Bringing deaths and injuries, massive destruction of property, and the interruption of normal law and order, war is the greatest violation of basic human rights that one people can inflict upon another. Starvation, exposure, and disease caused by war often produce more casualties than the fighting itself. War touches not only soldiers in battle and leaders in government but ordinary citizens—men, women, and children—as well.

Even as I write, thirty-four countries in the world are being torn apart by major civil wars. Many others are enduring lesser conflicts. Most of this fighting is taking place in poor and distant countries like Sri Lanka or Sudan. Since the American news media focus little attention on the poorer and less-developed nations of Asia, Africa, and South America, you may not hear about it on the nightly news or read about it in your local newspaper.

But because of these numerous bloody struggles, millions of people have lost their homes, livelihoods, and opportunities for medical care and education. Children in particular suffer— many do not know when to expect their next meal, whether they will ever attend school again, or where their parents might be. Thousands of children and teenagers have been placed in internment camps, and many others have been forced to serve as soldiers. Even though today our own nation is at peace, our global neighbors are feeling the ravages of war. As Americans and as fellow human beings, we must take action to help them find an end to the conflicts destroying their lives.

When I left the White House in 1981, my wife, Rosalynn, and I wanted to continue working for peace in the world. We founded the Carter Center, in Atlanta, Georgia, a private, non-political organization that tries to help countries resolve their internal conflicts in a peaceful manner. The center does this by encouraging individuals and governments to undertake peace talks instead of resorting to civil violence or military force, and, if possible, to hold free and fair democratic elections.

The Carter Center also tries to help citizens improve the quality of their lives during peacetime. Our programs are far-reaching: We teach farmers in Africa how to grow more food, we work with other international organizations to immunize children against deadly diseases, and we strive to stop human rights abuses among people who do not enjoy the political and civil rights Americans sometimes take for granted. Yet because none of these efforts can succeed in any country still torn by war, we also developed a special organization, the International Negotiation Network (INN), to study conflicts and ways to prevent or end them.

The INN monitors the major wars currently raging in the world. Much of this work is done by students at Emory University, who study government statements, news reports, and eyewitness accounts. Some of the students are able to attend conferences at the Carter Center, where leaders of warring parties come together for discussions. Through their work, these young people—mostly Americans, but also students from other nations often learn about a dispute directly from the people involved: its historical causes, the attitudes of the leaders, the goals of each side. They are able to observe how opposing parties begin to work together in search of a settlement that all sides can accept. Lessons drawn from this process often prove useful in understanding other conflicts.

In *Talking Peace,* you too will have a chance to explore conflict resolution. You will hear the inside story on how dialogues are initiated, how problems are addressed, and how solutions are reached. You will also consider some important questions: What basic living conditions are necessary for citizens in peacetime? Why do political leaders become more popular when they involve their nations in combat? How are food and medicine used as weapons in war? Why are innocent citizens in warring countries many more times as likely to die as soldiers? Why do some international peace efforts do more harm than good? Why is the United Nations so frequently unable to help? Why, in this country, are our cities and citizens—often our young people—torn by conflict, when as a nation we are at peace? Finally, how are you affected by all of this—and what can you do about it?

As president, I learned how difficult it is to bring together enemies who despise and distrust each other and whose goals or political beliefs are very different. Often, blood has been shed on both sides and lives lost, causing people to want revenge. Think about a time when you have had a bad disagreement with a friend or classmate, or perhaps someone in your own family. Do you remember how angry you felt when your opponent struck you or was particularly insulting? Did you want to stop the disagreement at that point, or did you prefer to fight back? In much the same way, once a disagreement has escalated, political leaders almost always find it easier and more popular to demonstrate their hatred for an enemy by aggressive language and combat rather than to support efforts for peace talks or for a cease-fire.

Peacemaking is not easy. In many ways, it is much more difficult than making war. But its great rewards cannot be measured in ordinary terms. In this book, I hope to share a little of what I have learned about the benefits of peace. And I hope to explain why we must not relax in our efforts to ease the pain and suffering caused by conflict and to help the world's people secure their safety, health, and freedoms.

As a young person entering the adult world, you will soon find you have inherited a planet in less than perfect shape. Yet many of us are working hard, every day, trying to ensure a better future for you. If you and your peers become more knowledgeable now about current conflicts, about the opportunities for successful conflict resolution, and about the shared blessings of peace, then we will have an even better chance of success. I hope you will join me, the team at the Carter Center, and many others around the world in waging peace.

You can and will make a difference!

TALKING PEACE

1

PEACE IN THE
MIDDLE EAST

Looking Back at Camp David

In January 1991, the United States went to war in the Middle East. Five months earlier, Saddam Hussein, dictator of Iraq, had sent his forces to occupy the small country of Kuwait. Kuwait is a major producer of petroleum, and when the invasion took place, many countries worried that the vital flow of Kuwaiti oil to the rest of the world would be interrupted. They also feared that Iraq planned to advance into other nearby nations, such as Saudi Arabia. The international community issued stern warnings and imposed economic sanctions on Iraq, but Hussein refused to yield. American troops led the United Nations coalition forces into battle, intending to force the Iraqi troops to withdraw.

Back at home, maps of the Middle East and videotaped footage of fighting filled the television news. Yellow ribbons tied around neighborhood trees across the country honored the American soldiers. You probably learned about the war in school and may have discussed it with your family at home. What led our country to defend a tiny kingdom so many thousands of miles away—a nation with fewer people than the state of Arkansas? And when Iraq surrendered just over a month later, what had we gained? Thousands of Iraqi soldiers and two hundred twenty-three American and other United Nations troops died. Over seven hundred oil wells were sabotaged or destroyed by the Iraqis, causing serious spillage and fumes that damaged the environment. Was this destruction really necessary? Was the war even successful?

These questions are not easy to answer. The military, economic, and cultural issues of the Middle East are extremely complex. When I was in the White House, I asked for a daily briefing from the CIA and the State Department to keep up with them.

What is known as the Middle East encompasses many countries: Israel, Iran, Iraq, Libya, Egypt, Jordan, Syria, Lebanon, Saudi Arabia, Yemen, Kuwait, Bahrain, Qatar, Oman, and the United Arab Emirates, as well as the Israeli occupied territories of the West Bank and the Gaza Strip. The different groups of people who live in the region are passionate about defending the territory and bodies of water they consider theirs. Often, their politics are very strongly influenced by their religious beliefs.

Home to many of the world's most ancient civilizations, the Middle East is also the birthplace of the three great monotheistic religions (those that recognize only one God): Judaism, Christianity, and Islam. Followers of each of these religions now live in many different countries throughout the world. For Jews, an ancient book called the Torah describes their early history and provides a basis for many of their cultural practices. Islamic believers, or Muslims, follow the teachings of the prophet Muhammad as recorded in a book called the Koran. The Koran prescribes common laws, a shared written language, and a universal Muslim culture. Christians find the history of Christ's life and teachings in the New Testament of the Bible. Tragically for the Middle East, the various interpretations of these holy books often cause disagreement and war rather than peace and healing.

The most highly publicized and perhaps the most important continuing conflict in the area is the dispute between Israel and its Arab neighbors regarding the territory historically known as Palestine. Palestine, which includes Israel itself and portions of bordering territories and countries, has been controlled by many different peoples over the centuries. The Ottoman Turks ruled the area from 1516 until their defeat in World War I, when Great Britain took over under a League of Nations mandate. At that time, two emerging national movements came into conflict, those of the Jews and the Arabs.

It was not until after World War II that the United Nations attempted to resolve this difficult situation, voting in 1947 to partition, or split, Palestine between the Jewish and Arab inhabitants. The new nation of Israel was born, but no Arab nation was willing to recognize its existence and make permanent peace. No separate Arab Palestinian state was established. The West Bank, including the city of Jerusalem, was taken over by

Jordan and the Gaza Strip by Egypt. Arab-Israeli conflict has continued on and off, with border skirmishes and full-scale wars in 1956, 1967, and 1973. Thousands have been killed on both sides.

At the end of the 1967 war, Israel took over territory that is recognized by the international community as belonging to

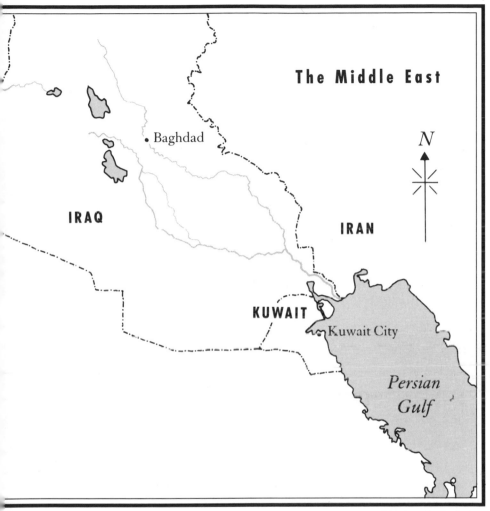

The Middle East

Baghdad

IRAQ

IRAN

N

KUWAIT

Kuwait City

Persian Gulf

Map by Claudia Carlson

Egypt, Syria, and the Palestinians. This land included the Sinai Peninsula of Egypt, the Golan Heights of Syria, and the West Bank and the Gaza Strip, areas inhabited mostly by Palestinians. It is important to understand why these people play such a crucial role in the continuing Middle East disputes.

The Palestinians are mostly Arabs whose families have lived

in what is now Israel, the West Bank, and the Gaza Strip for many generations. About 85 percent of them are Muslims and 15 percent are Christians. In the occupied territories, their affairs are now administered by Israeli civilian and military officials. Palestinians are treated as conquered people, forbidden to assemble for political purposes, to elect their own leaders, or to publicly criticize the Israeli government.

Increasingly during the past fifteen years, Jewish citizens of Israel have been encouraged by their leaders to settle in the occupied territories, especially in the neighborhoods around Jerusalem. Late in 1987, Palestinians living in the territories began an uprising called the intifada. In 1991, a series of peace talks was begun between Israel and various Arab states. These talks included the first face-to-face negotiations between the Palestinians and Israeli officials. Unfortunately, as of early 1993, the negotiations have not been fruitful. The arguments continuing today between Arabs and Jews have a long history behind them. Yet we must believe progress is possible.

Peace in the Middle East was a major concern for me and my administration, and our work in this area gave me much of my early experience in negotiation. At that time, the most serious confrontation was between Israel and Egypt, the most powerful Arab state. Probably our most highly publicized achievement was the Camp David Accords, an agreement that was later followed by a formal peace treaty between Israel and Egypt. The story of the accords provides dramatic proof that two enemies with a tradition of bloodshed between them can make a successful effort toward reconciliation.

SUMMIT AT CAMP DAVID

Shortly after my inauguration in 1977, President Anwar Sadat of Egypt came to visit me in Washington. He was interested in bringing peace to his own people and strengthening friendship between Egypt and the United States. However, he saw no chance to make real progress on resolving basic differences with Israel anytime soon. On several issues he responded, "Maybe in my lifetime." I told him that I was prepared to use my full personal influence and that of my country in support of any effort he was willing to make. Later, during our private talks upstairs in the White House, he agreed to take major strides toward peace in the long-standing conflict between his country and Israel. This was very much in the interest of the United States. (The last Israeli-Egyptian war, in 1973, had been the most recent time the Soviet and United States military forces had gone on nuclear alert.) Later, I met with Israeli Prime Minister Menachem Begin and found him willing to consider the initiatives Sadat and I had discussed.

In November 1977, Sadat made a dramatic trip to Israel to call for peace and to explain the demands of the Palestinian people living in the occupied territories. Although Begin and the members of the Israeli Knesset (parliament) listened politely, and although Begin personally repaid Sadat's visit, there were no concrete results from these overtures. I was disappointed at this lack of progress. One day, Rosalynn and I were walking down a woodland path at Camp David, the secluded presidential retreat in Maryland, talking about how beautiful and peaceful it was. Rosalynn said, "Jimmy, if we could only get Prime Minister Begin and President Sadat up here on this mountain

August 3, 1978

To Prime Minister Begin

This is a private and personal letter, and I would appreciate your honoring its confidentiality. I want to express myself frankly and directly to you personally.

During the past year under your leadership of Israel we have made remarkable progress toward peace. The boldness and leadership qualities exhibited by you and President Sadat have contributed to a new and better relationship between Israel and Egypt which was not anticipated by the rest of the world. In my opinion, you are the leader who, in the foreseeable future, can and must continue this progress. You have a strong hold on the government, loyalty among your associates, and the well deserved confidence of the people of your country.

It is imperative that every effort be made to capitalize on this unprecedented opportunity to consummate a definitive peace treaty between Israel and Egypt and then to match this achievement with other agreements between your nation and your other neighbors.

Although the recent discussions have produced minimal progress, broad areas of agreement do exist, providing a basis for sustained hope. Unless we take advantage of this opportunity now, however, those of us who presently serve as leaders of our respective nations may not again have such a chance to advance the cause of peace in the Middle East.

After hours of detailed discussions on several occasions with both you and President Sadat, in private and in group sessions, I am convinced of your mutual desire for peace. That desire is obviously shared by the people of both nations. Nevertheless, the high hopes of last winter have now been dissipated, with potentially serious consequences.

It is time, therefore, for a renewed effort at the highest level. My hope is that during this visit by Secretary Vance to the Middle East progress and harmony will be indicated by positive statements and the avoidance of public disputes.

Then, as soon as is convenient, I would like to meet personally with you and President Sadat to search for additional avenues toward peace.

Secretary Vance can discuss with you the arrangements for a time and place. Unnecessary delay would be a mistake. I have no strong preference about the location, but Camp David is available. My hope is that the three of us, along with our top advisors, can work together in relative seclusion. Maximum direct contact between you and President Sadat is very important.

To create the best climate for our meeting, public statements should be constructive and positive, expectations should not be raised too high, and quiet and mutual preparation should lay a foundation for optimum progress.

It is important that this proposal be kept completely confidential. President Sadat is being similarly approached. A time for announcement can be mutually set after we have fixed the date. Secretary Vance is familiar with my schedule, and I hope that through him you will send to me your ideas and advice.

I look forward to an early opportunity to consider with you again one of the most important and challenging issues ever decided by political leaders.

Please remember that you have my continuing friendship and personal best wishes as we work together as partners in a common search for peace.

Sincerely,
JIMMY CARTER

for a few days, I believe they might consider how they could prevent another war between their countries." That gave me the idea, and a few weeks later, I invited both men to join me for a series of private talks. In September 1978, they both came to Camp David.

On the agenda were several issues. Among the most important for Sadat were the Israeli occupation of Egyptian lands and the rights of Palestinians to their own homeland. Begin was most concerned about Israel's national security, about gaining formal diplomatic recognition from the Arab countries, and about the particular fate of Jerusalem—a holy place for Jew, Christian, and Muslim—if the occupied territories were to be relinquished or shared in some way. I hoped that in the process of the discussions we would answer many, or even all, of these questions.

My role as a mediator in the talks would be a challenge. To prepare, I studied thick books on the personalities of the two leaders, prepared for me by specialists in the United States intelligence services and the State Department. These books told me about each man's family relationships, religious beliefs, early experiences, health, and most important friends; also about how he had won office, how he responded to pressure, and what his hobbies and personal habits were. I took notes as I read that later proved very useful in the actual meetings. I also prepared lists of points on which the Egyptians and the Israelis were in apparent agreement, points of difference between them, questions to be asked during the negotiations, and some compromises I thought both men might accept.

Rosalynn would be at Camp David with me, and our advisers,

personal physicians, cooks, secretaries, and other assistants prepared to come for three days, or a little longer if necessary. We never imagined it would take thirteen long, hard days and nights before an agreement would finally be reached. The small mountain camp was not designed to accommodate so many people, particularly for such a length of time, and many special arrangements had to be made. The staff even had to prepare three different types of meals at each sitting—kosher food for Begin and the Israeli delegation; special food for Sadat, which his own personal chef would cook; and other food for the rest of us! We also planned to have three different religious services, using the same small room—for Muslims on Friday, for Jews on Saturday, and for Christians on Sunday.

President Sadat was the first to arrive for the peace talks, and I was pleased to discover that he seemed quite flexible on most questions. He said he was firm on the two issues of taking care of the Palestinian people and getting all Israeli settlers off the land in Egypt's Sinai Desert. In everything else, he would be willing to trust my judgment, and he agreed to stay at Camp David as long as necessary. Sadat voiced strong doubts about Begin's willingness to compromise. I urged him to consider the Israelis' caution in light of their special situation as a very small country surrounded by powerful and hostile Arab neighbors. When Prime Minister Begin arrived later, he and I also had a private discussion about the major issues.

Like Sadat, Begin was a man of deep religious beliefs. When he mentioned places in the Middle East, he called them by their biblical names. He felt the historical import of our talks and wanted very much to insure a safe future for the Jewish people.

Yet I soon realized that he viewed our Camp David sessions as just the first in a long series of negotiations, while Sadat and I had hoped to settle all the major controversial issues between the two countries during the next few days, if we possibly could. True to his initial approach, Begin would prove to be extremely cautious about details, examining every word in any text we might consider.

During the discussions, the three of us kept to our different personal styles. Begin dressed in business suits, wearing a tie at all times. He worked long hours, generally with his own advisers, and usually ate his meals in the main hall with the Israeli, Egyptian, and American delegations. For recreation, he liked to read or play chess. Sadat wore stylish sports clothes and followed a strict personal regimen, caring for his diet, sleep, and exercise. He ate privately in his cottage and took long, fast walks each morning. I usually wore jeans, a sports shirt, and running shoes, and ate in the dining hall or in our cabin with Rosalynn. For an hour or two during the late afternoon, some of us, mostly Americans, usually swam, jogged, or played tennis. In between negotiating sessions, I would go over notes of previous meetings or prepare for the next session with help from an American team from the White House and the State Department.

From the first day, we worked on the problem of the West Bank and the Gaza Strip. We had to discuss the Israelis' claim that they had occupied these places in 1967 in an attempt to defend themselves against a war the Arabs had started, and that they were therefore entitled to keep at least part of the area. Egypt's argument was that the territory had been seized illegally, and that all of it should be returned to its original owners, the Palestinians. If Israel did agree to release the land, we also had to discuss how the Palestinians could then govern themselves without threatening Israel's sense of security.

As we discussed these and other emotional issues, I soon realized that Begin and Sadat were personally incompatible. The sometimes petty, sometimes heated arguments that arose between them when we were all in the same room convinced me it would be better if each of them spoke to me as the mediator instead of directly to the other. Each of the two leaders accused the other of trying to destroy his country's economy and even deliberately encouraging the illegal trade in hashish and other drugs. For the last ten days of the Camp David negotiations, the two men never spoke to or even saw each other except for a Sunday afternoon trip to the nearby Civil War battlefield at Gettysburg, although their teams of advisers did continue to meet face-to-face.

I went back and forth between the two leaders and their advisers, constantly seeking approval on the wording of each point of a comprehensive agreement. It was a slow and tedious process, and all of us were often discouraged, seeing little or no chance for success. Toward the end of the talks, Begin's foreign minister told Sadat that Israel would never compromise on certain major issues, and Sadat decided to leave. The Egyptians packed their bags and asked for a helicopter to take them to Washington so they could return home. When I heard about this, I said a silent prayer, quickly changed into more formal clothes, and went to confront Sadat in his cabin. After an intense argument in which I reminded him of his promises to me and stressed the global importance of his role as a man of peace, Sadat agreed to give the process another chance.

Each day I would write down a list of the points on which

agreement had been reached, with a separate list of outstanding differences. Slowly but surely, the second list got smaller and smaller.

Sadat's insistence that all Israeli families must leave the Sinai Peninsula was a sticking point for Begin. I knew it would be hard, if not impossible, for Begin to agree to this Egyptian demand. He believed the Jews had a right to stay in the area and had promised his people not to dismantle any Israeli settlements. Sadat would tell me that Begin wanted land instead of peace; Begin would say that Sadat wanted the land to prepare for another war against Israel. During the first three days they were together, there were personal attacks, sometimes embarrassing for me to witness. When the two men were at a stalemate, I would try to negotiate with their advisers instead.

Day after day, assisted by my American advisers, I revised and presented new drafts of the agreement to both negotiating teams. On the eleventh day, however, I finally realized we faced failure because of just two issues: the dismantling of Israeli settlements in the Sinai and the status of the city of Jerusalem. We had negotiated a good paragraph about sharing control of the holy city, but it was such an emotional issue for both Jews and Muslims that both Begin and Sadat became nervous about how their countries would react if they included the paragraph in the final document. Even if we compromised by leaving the question of Jerusalem out of the agreement, it was apparent that neither man intended to compromise on settlements in the Sinai. At this point, I had been away from Washington and the nation's business for a long time. I informed everyone that I would have to return to the White House on Sunday, the thirteenth day, and this ultimatum fixed a final deadline for our talks.

In the end, something unexpected almost miraculously helped to break the deadlock. We had made some photos of the three of us, and Begin had asked me to sign one for each of his eight grandchildren. Sadat had already signed them. My secretary suggested that I personalize them, and on each photograph I wrote in the name of one grandchild above my signature. Although Begin had become quite unfriendly toward me because of the pressure I was putting on him and Sadat, I decided to take the photographs over to his cabin personally. As he looked at the pictures and read the names aloud, he became very emotional. He was thinking, I am sure, about his responsibility to his people and about what happens to children in war. Both of us had tears in our eyes. He promised to review the language of my latest revisions.

Shortly thereafter, Begin called me. He would accept my compromise proposal, which was to leave the decision about dismantling the settlements up to the Israeli parliament. I had thought of this as a way out for him. He would not have to back down on his promise not to dismantle any Israeli settlements but could shift the burden of the decision to the parliament. It worked. The American team struggled frantically to get a final draft of what would become the Camp David Accords, incorporating all the last-minute changes, which Sadat and Begin finally both approved. This was, indeed, a framework for peace, as we called it, laying the foundation for a future treaty between Israel and Egypt.

When I realized we had succeeded at last, I immediately called Rosalynn, who had given me support and advice during the long Camp David negotiations but had returned to the White House earlier that day. With the final document approved, Begin walked over to Sadat's cabin, about one hundred yards away, and the two men met again for the first time in days and shook hands as friends.

That afternoon, Begin, Sadat, and I left Camp David in my helicopter and flew to the White House for the signing ceremony. Six months later, after Israeli settlers had begun withdrawing from Egypt's Sinai region, a formal treaty was signed between the two countries—the first treaty ever between Israel and an Arab nation. Since that time, the Camp David Accords have provided guidance to other negotiators, and the treaty has stood as a bulwark against major conflict in the region. Fighting has claimed many lives in the occupied territories over the future of the Palestinians, but Egypt and Israel have continued to honor the specific stipulations of the March 1979 agreement.

THE MIDDLE EAST TODAY

Although most Americans supported our military attack on Iraq in 1991, I strongly urged at the time that peaceful options be exhausted first. I know how difficult it is for nations in dispute to agree to negotiations once a confrontation exists and abusive public statements have been made. As with Begin and Sadat, extraordinary courage is often required on the part of political leaders to speak out against what might be perceived as the wave of popular sentiment in favor of war. Although both men won the Nobel Peace Prize for their peace agreement, Sadat was later assassinated because of the unpopularity of his positions with the more extreme Muslim factions.

Was the Persian Gulf War necessary? We can only guess about what might have happened if a sincere effort had been made to resolve the major issues through negotiation. Was the

When I first saw Kuwait City following its liberation by United Nations forces, I couldn't believe how much damage had been done during the city's occupation and during the fight to free it from the Iraqi invaders. I could tell that it had once been a beautiful place, with well-kept gardens between rows of modern Western-style buildings that looked out over the Persian Gulf.

What it looked like in early March 1991 was something out of a horror movie. Most of the buildings were destroyed. Burned-out cars, trucks, and military vehicles littered the streets. There was no clean water or fresh food for the people. Garbage and debris were scattered everywhere, and dogs and cats that had been people's pets only a few weeks before scavenged for scraps in the piles of refuse. As I drove down the streets, surveying the damage, dozens of children ran out of the ruins that had been their homes to beg for food. They had the hollow looks on their faces that came from seeing the horrors of war firsthand. They were hungry and desperate. Many of them had surely lost their parents and brothers and sisters. Most had nowhere to live.

What had these children done to deserve what had happened to them and their families? Nothing. Their only crime was being born in the wrong place at the wrong time. When I remember them now, I think of the opportunities that almost every American child has. I hope that as Americans, we can all work together to achieve everything that we dream, and that someday all the children in the world can share in the gift of freedom that we so often take for granted.

JIM JOHNSON
a young United States Army National Guard officer who participated in the Persian Gulf War

war truly successful? We must consider that as I write this book, Saddam Hussein is still in power, and Iraq may still have nuclear capabilities. Both during and since the war, Iraqi troops have killed thousands of Kurdish tribespeople, who oppose Saddam's dictatorship and demand their own self-government. Possibly two million Kurds and Shiites (a Muslim sect that is in conflict with Saddam Hussein's Ba'th Socialist Party) have been displaced from their homes.

Looking back on the Camp David process, it is easy to understand how difficult negotiated conflict resolution can be. Political and military leaders are always convinced that their particular war is justified. Religion, greed, a thirst for power or land, loyalty to allies, the desire to alleviate suffering among their people, ancient grievances to be settled—any or all of these reasons can persuade leaders to go to war. Yet looking at the progress that was made as a result of the Camp David Accords, the Israeli-Egyptian peace treaty, and the completion of the Israeli withdrawal from the Sinai in 1982, it is also easy to see how advantageous a nonviolent settlement to a conflict can be.

In the Middle East, many issues remain unresolved. What happens to the people of this troubled region will have a direct effect on our own lives. Not only could war rapidly increase the price of oil and all its products, causing severe damage to the American economy, but, as with disturbances in other regions, our nation could once again be dragged into armed combat.

2

WAGING PEACE

A Personal Commitment

It is one thing to say that we each have the right not to be killed. It is another to say that we each have the right to live comfortably, with adequate food, health care, shelter, education, and opportunities for employment. It is even more powerful to say that we each have the right to worship as we choose, to say what we choose, and to be governed by leaders we choose. And perhaps the most powerful statement of all is to say that we each hold these rights equally—that no one person is more entitled to any of these rights than the next, regardless of his or her sex, race, or station in life.

When I was preparing for the presidency, I thought very hard about what human rights meant to me. I studied what previous presidents had believed, and learned that our nation has always been strongest when we have lived up to our founding ideals —advocating life, liberty, and the pursuit of happiness, not just for ourselves but for others. Our commitment to basic human principles strengthens our ties with allies and our influence in the world. In my inaugural address, I said, "Because we are free, we can never be indifferent to the fate of freedom elsewhere."

In the area of human rights, the United States is the natural leader among the world's more than one hundred seventy-five countries. We were the first nation to be founded upon these ideals. We have never been perfect in our observance of human rights, but throughout our history we have consistently expanded our understanding of what human rights mean. By supporting international efforts to prosecute human rights violators and by our foreign policy, the United States can encourage a focus on human rights around the world.

When we think about what our country can do to raise the quality of life for other people, we also must look at our own history. The struggle by African-Americans for civil rights was one of the longest and most difficult tests our country has yet seen. When people ask me where my first interest in human rights began, I usually tell them about my childhood in Georgia, where I lived in a segregated society.

Between 1865 and 1870, the United States Constitution was amended to abolish slavery and then to guarantee equal rights, including the right to vote, to all citizens. However, in 1896, the Supreme Court ruled that railroads could require black and white passengers to occupy separate coaches, provided the accommodations were of equal quality. After that time, this "separate but equal" ruling was abused to permit gross discrimination against African-Americans. In all southern states black citizens were required to go to separate schools and prevented from drinking at the same water fountains, using the same rest rooms, or even ordering a sandwich from the same lunch counters as white customers.

When I was a child, almost all our neighbors were black, and the children were my playmates. When not in school or church we treated one another as complete equals in our games, as we did while fishing or working in the field. As we grew older, however, we came to realize that we lived in a segregated society. Recently, I wrote a poem about how this happened to me and my two friends, A.D. and Johnny.

THE PASTURE GATE

This empty house three miles from town
was where I lived. Here I was back,
and found most homes around were gone.
The folks who stayed here now were black,
like Johnny and A.D., my friends.

As boys we worked in Daddy's fields,
hunted rabbits, squirrels, and quail,
caught and cooked catfish and eels,
searched the land for arrowheads,
tried to fly the smallest kite,
steered barrel hoops with strands of wire,
and wrestled hard. At times we'd fight,
without a thought who might be boss,

who was smartest or the best;
the leader for a few brief hours
was who had won the last contest.

But then—we were fourteen or so—
as we approached the pasture gate,
they went to open it, and then
stood back. This made me hesitate,
sure it must have been a joke,
a trip wire, maybe, they had planned.
I reckon they had to obey
their parents' prompting. Or command.
We saw it only vaguely then,
but we were transformed at that place.
A silent line was drawn between
friend and friend, race and race.

Although I was aware that my position in our community was more privileged than that of my black playmates, no one I knew ever talked openly in public about trying to equalize the different standards of living between the two races.

More than anyone else, my mother made me see the inequalities around us. She was a registered nurse living on our farm near Plains, Georgia, during the Great Depression, and was often called upon to help poverty-stricken neighbors, both black and white, when there was no medical doctor. She worked as a nurse for as many as twenty hours a day, often for little or no pay, without regard to her patients' race or social status. My mother's quiet service to others, regardless of their race or social position, was a good lesson for me. Later, as a submarine officer,

I was influenced by the policies of President Harry Truman, who sought to abolish racial discrimination in the United States armed forces.

I resigned from the U.S. Navy and returned to Plains in 1953. A year later, in *Brown v. Board of Education,* the "separate but equal" ruling was overturned by the U.S. Supreme Court, whose members voted unanimously to prohibit racial segregation in the public schools. In 1955, a black woman named Rosa Parks refused to move to the back of a bus in Montgomery, Alabama. In supporting her, a young minister named Martin Luther King, Jr., brought dramatic new leadership to the civil rights movement. Additional progress was made when more than seventy thousand black and white college and high school students joined the effort by supporting sit-ins at lunch counters and restaurants throughout the South.

It was still almost impossible to change state segregation laws, because many of those who held elected office at that time preferred the system the way it was. Unfair, outdated electoral laws helped prevent reform. The weight of votes was determined by counties instead of by individuals. This meant that in certain small counties, a person's vote counted almost one hundred times as much as a vote in a large city. Elections for state legislators, governors, and other officials were decided by small rural counties, where black citizens were discouraged from registering to vote and most ballots were cast by conservative whites. But another landmark Supreme Court decision, known as the one man, one vote ruling, came in 1962. This decision required that every person's vote in an election should be given approximately the same weight. (As a result of this ruling, I decided to run for state senate. In 1992, I wrote a book called *Turning Point,* which describes this change in my own life, in Georgia, and in our nation.)

A far-reaching civil rights bill, outlawing discrimination in public places and in employment practices, was passed by the U.S. Congress in 1964. And the following year, Congress passed the Voting Rights Act, further protecting citizens against racial discrimination. Now that these major legal issues were resolved, the long and bitter struggle over race could be moved into the background of our lives, and we black and white citizens could begin to work and enjoy ourselves together as neighbors.

Unfortunately, although laws had been changed, racism was still prevalent among our people. Many white parents refused to let their children attend the integrated schools or participate in social or sporting events where black and white young people were together. A large number of private schools known as segregation academies were established in the South, where all-white teachers instructed all-white students.

When I was inaugurated as governor of Georgia in 1971, I announced, "The time for racial discrimination is over." When I ordered that the portrait of Dr. Martin Luther King, Jr., be hung in the state capitol to honor him as one of Georgia's heroes, members of the Ku Klux Klan marched around the building in protest. Today, some twenty years later, Georgians are overwhelmingly proud of their progress toward racial equality. However, issues related to race remain difficult to resolve in my state and throughout our nation.

I first focused on international human rights when I became a candidate in the 1976 presidential election. As I spoke to voters, I learned how disillusioned the general public had become with the Vietnam War. Many American citizens also let me know about persecution of their relatives who still lived in foreign countries. When I was elected, it was natural for my administration to listen to the people and focus on the issues of peace and human rights.

The existence of war is incompatible with our basic needs as human beings: a stable home, food and health care, a life free from fear and persecution. The tragedy is that often most national leaders and the news media pay little attention to conflicts around the world until wars cause such destruction and starvation that they can be ignored no longer. We hoped that our human rights emphasis would draw attention to those people who were suffering from the pain of conflict, many of whom did not have a peaceful outlet to voice their outrage and despair.

When Rosalynn and I left the White House, we returned to our home in Plains, Georgia. One of my first responsibilities was to build a presidential library. Since the retirement of Harry Truman, former presidents have been expected to provide such a place to house all their administration's records and documents, the official history of our country for the time each served as president. I struggled with the design and the difficult task of raising the money to pay for the construction. I was very concerned about building a library that would function not merely as a memorial to my administration but would be a workplace that would serve some greater purpose in the world. I would also have to make a living for my family. I was not ready for retirement!

How could I use my experience as governor and president to build an organization where I could address some of the issues in which I had the most interest, especially peace and human rights? Rosalynn remembers that I woke up in the middle of the night during this difficult time of transition and talked to her about building a center near the library where she and I could work on conflict resolution and some of the other issues that were important to us while I was president. Perhaps we could even tie this center to a university, where I could get a job teaching.

From that midnight discussion came plans for the Carter Center, which would become a private, nonprofit organization associated closely with Emory University, in Atlanta. It would be located adjacent to the presidential library, which, once built, would be owned and operated by the United States National Archives and Records Administration.

At the center, I planned again to address the issues of education, health, the environment, human rights, and, of course, global conflict. Most of all, I wanted the Carter Center to be a place where people from all walks of life and all religious and ethnic backgrounds could come to seek peaceful resolutions to troubling and complicated problems.

Before we finalized the architect's layout and followed through with the construction of the buildings, I had decided upon a few important guidelines for our work, which we have followed from the center's very earliest days. First of all, we are careful not to duplicate what is already being done by others. If the United Nations, the United States government, the World Bank, or a major university is making good progress on a problem, we do not compete with them. Second, we only undertake projects leading to direct action that will benefit people's lives. Just doing academic research is not our role, no matter how important or interesting a subject might be. Another im-

About the Carter Center

Some of the world's problems are so difficult that no individual or institution alone can solve them. There are many caring people and good organizations working to bring warring parties to peace, to immunize children, and to combat human rights abuses. Former President Jimmy Carter knew that by combining these efforts, more problems could be solved and the world could be a better place to live. The product of that vision is the Carter Center.

When was the Carter Center founded?

The center was founded in 1982 by Jimmy and Rosalynn Carter on the campus of Emory University, in Atlanta. In 1986, the Carter Center moved to new facilities, along with the Jimmy Carter Library and Museum. The center maintains its affiliation with Emory, which is located a few miles away.

What is the center's mission?

The Carter Center is founded on the principle that everyone on earth should be able to live in peace. In pursuit of this goal, the center has earned an international reputation for bringing people and resources together to resolve conflict, foster democracy and development, and fight hunger, disease, and human rights abuses. By seeking ways to meet basic human needs, the center draws on President Carter's access to world leaders and forms partnerships with other institutions and individuals to achieve larger goals.

Some of the center's recent accomplishments include:

- Monitoring democratic elections in Panama, Nicaragua, Zambia, Haiti, Guyana, and other countries.

- Tracking armed conflicts within and between nations around the world and offering assistance in dispute resolution.
- Protecting and promoting human rights and supporting the emergence of free print and broadcast media, especially in countries undergoing a transition to democracy.
- Helping increase the immunization rate of the world's children from 20 percent to 80 percent in five years.
- Assisting one hundred fifty thousand families in Ghana, Nigeria, Togo, Benin, and Tanzania increase food production by conducting agricultural training programs.
- Fighting river blindness, a disease spread by blackflies, by distributing the drug Mectizan to twenty-six African nations.
- Preventing guinea worm disease by distributing water filters and supporting other water purification efforts.
- Promoting better understanding between the United States and the former Soviet Union by cofounding the American Law Center, in Moscow.
- Launching a comprehensive effort, through the Atlanta Project, to alleviate the problems associated with urban poverty.
- Working to erase the stigma associated with mental illness and to fight discrimination against mental illness in the health care system.

portant rule is that our center is nonpartisan, with Democrats, Republicans, and others working together on the same team.

As the Carter Center's programs have fallen into place, we have carefully assembled a staff of experts, led by scholars whom we call fellows. As we take on each new project, one of our fellows works with other scholars to do a study of the issue or problem. Then we bring together experts and strong leaders from all over the world who have practical experience and can put into action the ideas and recommendations that might be forthcoming from the study. When necessary, we recruit qualified people to work full-time on the project, in the United States or in other countries.

The Carter Center also offers an internship program for students from Emory University and other colleges. Approximately one hundred interns work on Carter Center projects each academic year, conducting research on world conflicts, monitoring human rights abuses, and assisting in the planning of conferences and consultations held at the center. Most of them receive academic credit for their work, and many anticipate an international career of their own in the future.

It is likely that the Carter Center will expand its present work by cooperating more fully with the governments of the United States and other countries and with international and private agencies. There are many roles these institutions cannot play by themselves in preventing or resolving civil wars, holding democratic elections, exposing and correcting human rights violations, and alleviating the suffering of people who are hungry, homeless, or lack medical care. Our center is very flexible in changing its tasks and therefore able to act quickly to meet new challenges. Increasingly, we will combine our own programs with those of Emory University, so that the knowledge of scholars and scientists can be beneficial to people in need, and our staff's practical experiences in foreign countries and America's inner cities can be channeled back into research and teaching to enrich the lives of students and professors.

When I became executive director of the Carter Center in early 1993, I stepped into a leadership role in an organization unlike any other in the world. The center is unique because it has a former U.S. president at its helm, but also because it is very effective at building partnerships among peoples of the world and sharing information that can improve, even save, lives.

As a physician, I know the great difference that scientific knowledge, when applied in the right way, can have on a society. That's why, in 1990, I traveled to Geneva, Switzerland, where the Carter Center was initiating an antitobacco campaign with the World Health Organization (WHO). Most children in the United States know that tobacco kills. At home and in school, they are taught about the dangers of smoking. The U.S. government even mandates that cigarette packages and ads carry warning labels about the health hazards of smoking—warnings based on scientific evidence about the damage tobacco does to the human body. Tobacco is one of the few products that, when used as directed, can kill you. Yet, even in the United States, where teachers and parents try to keep youths from harming themselves in this way, 85 to 90 percent of all smokers start by age twenty.

In the last ten years, when the number of smokers in the United States began to decrease, tobacco companies began to look in the developing world for new customers for their products. The number of young people who smoke in Africa and Asia is increasing, because advertising convinces them that smoking is sexy, glamorous, and exciting. Billboards and magazine ads don't tell them that they might someday be one of the three million people killed each year from smoking.

The companies that make cigarettes need to admit the detrimental effect their products have on the health of the world's children and young adults, and then do something to change that. Until then, we must educate each other and find creative ways to eliminate this killer. For example, the Carter Center, working with WHO, has built partnerships with governments in the African countries of Namibia, Kenya, and the Congo to deter tobacco use through education and by drafting laws that eliminate tobacco ads, increase the taxes countries pay to import tobacco products, make it illegal to sell cigarettes to minors, or increase the price of tobacco.

Smoking is a hard habit to break, and no one can do it alone. Only by working together with our friends across the street, in other schools, communities, states, and countries, can we build a tobacco-free world.

Dr. John Hardman
executive director of the Carter Center

3

MAKING WAR

Centuries of Conflict

Those who study and seek peace in any age quickly come to understand that war has been a fundamental force in human history. In the first chapter, we learned a little about some of the conflicts that have taken place in the Middle East during the past fifty years. But battles have raged there and in other regions since biblical times, and even before. The history of conflict is as old as humanity itself.

On the most basic level, conflict occurs when interests differ. As soon as two or more groups exist in a situation, there are two or more points of view—and two or more sets of ambitions as well. While sometimes each group can pursue its own ambitions without interfering with the other's, quite often conflicts will arise. The peacemaker's job is to settle differences through compromise and negotiation before they erupt into violence.

Conflicting views do not necessarily lead to fighting. War is merely one form of resolving conflict, a violent form. Nonviolent alternatives include negotiation and mediation to reach compromises and passive civil disobedience to emphasize and publicize the absence of agreement. This was how the American civil rights movement forced an end to legalized racial discrimination. But for various reasons at different times, hundreds of leaders in the history of the world have felt that war was an appropriate and justified means to resolve a conflict.

The reasons for going to war are many and varied. Battles may occur because a piece of land that has long been related to one group is taken over or controlled by another. Nations struggle over natural resources, including access to seas and oceans. Historically, ideas also have led to war. When one group has no tolerance for the religious opinions, race, or ethnicity of its neighbors, violent conflict can erupt. A change in the politics of a government that harms the average citizen's quality of life may inspire war. An oppressive regime's abuse of the people may eventually incite protest or outright rebellion.

In 1775, American colonial leaders chose armed resistance to the British monarchy in order to protect what they considered to be their rights of self-government. When the British government refused to yield, the conflict became a war for independence. Shortly before the battle at Lexington, which began the American Revolution, Patrick Henry made his famous statement of resolve, "I know not what course others may take; but as for me, give me liberty, or give me death!" Another advocate of the Revolution, Thomas Paine, later said, "It is the object only of a war that makes it honorable. And if there was ever a just war since the world began, it is this in which America is now engaged." Few Americans today would criticize the military actions our forefathers took to liberate America from British rule and to support democratic ideals for all people.

Though it is often obvious why one country would want to escape another's domination, it is sometimes harder to explain why citizens of a single country begin fighting among themselves in a civil war. It would seem that two peoples living close together would be more sympathetic toward each other and less likely to go to war. Time and time again, civil wars have erupted, proving that this theory is not true.

Almost ninety years after the revolution against the British, we Americans experienced our own civil war, as states and even members of the same families fought against one another. The causes of this tragic War Between the States were complicated. Among them were the struggle to abolish slavery, the assertion by certain states of their right to withdraw from the Union, and the domination of the northern states' industrial economy over the South's traditional agricultural way of life. After four years of bloody conflict and tragic loss, slavery was abolished and the Union was preserved. But as with most wars, the question remains: Could these goals have been reached peacefully?

There is no way to rewrite history, but who knows what would have happened if negotiation between distinguished and respected leaders had resolved the basic differences between North and South concerning the abolition of slavery and the elimination of what the South considered to be unfair economic discrimination against its region. Was there some peaceful alternative to the war's destruction and the hundreds of thousands of battlefield deaths? Although we will never know, we can apply the same kinds of questions to modern-day threats to peace.

Historians who study why leaders are willing to risk battle have found that usually one of two conditions exists: Either the leaders are highly confident that they will win, or they are more concerned about what will happen to them if they do *not* fight than if they do. Since the invention of massively destructive nuclear weapons earlier this century, many people felt that no leader would ever consider the risks of war to be worth it again. Yet smaller wars continue to explode all over the globe. This is in part because our human history of thousands of past wars sets a strong precedent.

It would be very difficult to explore all of the history of war within the scope of this book, but it is important to remember that as the nature of warfare itself has changed, opinions on the morality and advisability of war have also changed.

Despite the promise of the Hebrew prophet Isaiah some twenty-seven hundred years ago that a time would come when "nation shall not lift up sword against nation, neither shall they learn war any more," few nations have abandoned war as a means of advancing their interests. In the ancient world, few moral limits were placed on the conduct of war. When an army of Egypt, Assyria, Rome, or the ancient Israelites conquered a city, the soldiers believed their gods gave them the right to loot the city and to kill or enslave their captives.

Nations did develop ways of avoiding war through diplomacy, however. The Greek city-states, especially, cultivated the arts of negotiation and arbitration, usually to form beneficial alliances. Also, rules of warfare evolved. In Christian Europe during the Middle Ages, knights followed the customs of chivalry when they fought among themselves. However, their rules on how to treat their rival knights were not observed when they fought against people of different religions, such as the Muslims.

In the seventeenth and eighteenth centuries, advances in knowledge and science brought changes to the conduct of war and to attitudes about war. Weapons grew more destructive as the technology for using gunpowder improved. Nations began to see the military as a job for professionals who could apply scientific knowledge to make war efficient. At the same time, new ideas were in the air about the responsibilities and rights of human beings and of nation-states.

Some nations in western Europe were coming to the conclusion that limits needed to be placed on war. They considered it criminal to murder or enslave the civilian population of an occupied territory. There was, and continues to be, much disagreement about what is required by international law. However, the advocates of international law have had a significant influence on establishing more humane standards for the conduct of wars between nations. Unfortunately, these guidelines are often ignored by leaders who wage war against their own people.

Early in the twentieth century, the leading nations of Europe became embroiled in World War I, which proved to be more costly and destructive that any previous war in history. The military strategists were slow to adjust to the more powerful weapons at their disposal. Soldiers were slaughtered by the thousands as they attempted frontal assaults against the exploding shells and rapid-fire weapons of their entrenched enemies. Even though the nations engaged in the war recognized that civilians should be treated differently than soldiers, some of the new weapons made it difficult to follow the rules of war that had developed. The submarine is one example. When a surface naval warship caught an unarmed or lightly armed enemy merchant ship, it was required to give the merchant ship the opportunity to surrender. But when a submarine caught an enemy ship, it had to rely on a surprise attack for effectiveness. The merchant ship might be able to outrun the submarine if able to detect it. The outrage caused by German submarine attacks on American and British merchant ships with American civilian passengers on board ultimately helped bring the United States into the war against Germany.

The danger to civilian populations increased even more with the outbreak of World War II. Airplanes sent to bomb military targets often hit civilians as well. Both sides in the war conducted deliberate air raids on the cities of their enemies, and the Germans also launched missiles at Great Britain strictly to terrorize the British people. German treatment of Jewish civilian populations in Germany and in occupied territories included mass murders and enslavement in labor camps. After the war, some German leaders were convicted of war crimes. High civilian casualties were inevitable when the United States dropped the atomic bomb on Japan. The first bomb dropped on Hiroshima destroyed or severely damaged 98 percent of the buildings in the city's center. Of the city's three hundred fifty thousand inhabitants, seventy-one thousand were killed by the blast. Within five years, the effects of radiation brought the death toll to an estimated two hundred thousand people. President Harry Truman explained that many more than twice this number would have perished with prolonged conventional bombing and a military invasion of Japan.

The terrible threat of nuclear weapons may be the most

One of our most harrowing experiences came quickly. After five days of being on exhibit in towns and villages behind the front, we were marched one afternoon to a rail yard and loaded into forty-eight boxcars. In my car, we were joined by others for a total of probably more than two hundred prisoners, packed in until there was literally not enough room for everyone to lie down. We had to take turns or else sit propped up against the sides of the car.

There was no heat; there were no toilet facilities; there was no food, and no water except the little that was in our canteens when we boarded. It was bitterly cold, although at least we still had our new winter uniforms. The cold was enough to make us miserable,

important reason that no other world wars have occurred since 1945. The hope of many of the world's people was that the United Nations would prevent war. Its charter, created in 1945, prescribes that "all members shall refrain in their international relations from the threat or use of force against the territorial integrity or political independence of any state, or in any other manner inconsistent with the purposes of the United Nations." Unfortunately, soon after its establishment, increasing hostility developed between the two superpowers, the United States and the Soviet Union.

The building up of nuclear arsenals by the superpowers and the three other permanent members of the Security Council (China, Great Britain, and France) made the organization incapable of fulfilling its potential. Under the UN charter, any decision of the Security Council can be blocked by the veto of just one of these five. Since practically all important issues affect

but it would have been bearable if there had not been other indignities.

Some of the men now had severe diarrhea. Helmet liners and helmets were put into service as chamber pots. The stench was terrible, but the pitiable condition of the sick GI's was worse. They became dehydrated, and the little water we had was soon gone. The cracks in the walls of the boxcar became a blessing in disguise —at least we could reach through and get enough snow to stave off acute thirst. Without food or medicine, the sick got sicker, and before our ride was over, several died, including one in our car.

WILLIAM WATSON
an American soldier in World War II
who was a German prisoner of war

one of these major powers or its allies, the United Nations became relatively ineffective in making or implementing decisions. The United States and its allies, and the Soviet Union and its allies, engaged in a cold war. They saw each other as the enemy and threatened massive retaliation if the other dared to strike first.

Until the cold war, the globe had never before been split so neatly between the influence of two powers. According to some analysts, the superpowers' arms race and rhetoric succeeded in deterring a major war because there was always relative equality between the two countries militarily and economically. At no point did either side feel truly confident in its ability to win a war against the other.

Beginning in 1985, President Mikhail Gorbachev brought dramatic reform to the Soviet Union. The consequences were revolutionary. The end of Communist domination of the government, freedom of speech, economic reforms, a reduction of Soviet influence in neighboring countries, and the eventual breakup of the Soviet Union into more than a dozen independent countries brought an end to the cold war by 1990.

The cold war definitely had a major impact on the rest of the world, whether or not it was the only way the two superpowers could have saved themselves from mutual destruction. The race for arms and the great diversion of financial resources it required had a huge effect on the stability of the poorer nations, which as a group have seen more small wars among themselves during these last fifty years than at any point in history.

Throughout this period there was a ready supply of armaments, even to the poorest countries. In recent years, almost $1 trillion was spent in the world annually on weapons or the preparation for war. This dramatically reduced the funding available for alleviating human suffering and made people desperate and angry in their poverty. Military leaders in these poor countries received most of the money and benefits from outside sources, and they either took over the governments or dominated civilian leaders and deprived them of power. Without real democracy, human rights abuses tend to increase, providing another reason for people in a country to fight one another. In certain cases the United States and the Soviet Union contributed to these wars either by supplying armaments and aid, whether openly or covertly, or by engaging in the fighting itself.

It is surprising how many times the United States has been involved in combat just during my lifetime. World War II in the 1940s was followed by the Korean War in the 1950s, the Vietnam War in the 1960s and 1970s, and the sponsorship of the Contra War in Nicaragua and the invasions of Grenada and

Instances of the Use of United States Armed Forces Abroad

JANUARY 1977 TO JANUARY 1993

Administration of Jimmy Carter · January 1977–January 1981

1978 Zaire
U.S. military aircraft provided logistical support to Belgian and French rescue operations.

1980 Iran
Six U.S. transport planes and eight helicopters were used in an attempt to rescue American hostages.

Administration of Ronald Reagan · January 1981–January 1989

1981 El Salvador
Additional U.S. military advisers were sent to assist in training government forces in counterinsurgency.

1981 Libya
U.S. planes shot down two Libyan jets over the Gulf of Sidra after one of them had fired a heat-seeking missile.

1982 Sinai
Military personnel and equipment were deployed to participate in the multinational force in the Sinai.

1982   Lebanon

Eighty marines served in the multinational force to assist in the withdrawal of Palestine Liberation forces from Beirut.

1982   Lebanon

Twelve hundred marines served in a temporary multinational force to facilitate the restoration of Lebanese government sovereignty.

1983   Egypt

After a Libyan plane bombed a city in Sudan, the U.S. dispatched an AWACS electronic plane to Egypt.

1983   Honduras

The U.S. undertook a series of exercises in Honduras that some believed might lead to conflict with Nicaragua.

1983   Chad

Two AWACS electronic surveillance planes and eight F-15 fighter planes were deployed to assist Chad against Libyan and rebel forces.

1983   Grenada

Marine and army airborne troops landed on Grenada to protect lives and assist in the restoration of law and order.

1984   Persian Gulf

Aided by U.S. intelligence and fueled by a U.S. KC-10 tanker, Saudi Arabian jet fighter planes shot down two Iranian fighter planes over the Persian Gulf.

1985 Italy

U.S. Navy pilots intercepted an Egyptian airliner that was carrying the hijackers of the Italian cruise ship the *Achille Lauro*.

1986 Honduras

Unarmed U.S. military helicopters and crewmen ferried Honduran troops to the Nicaraguan border to repel Nicaraguan troops.

1986 Libya

U.S. forces, while engaged in freedom-of-navigation exercises, were attacked by Libyan missiles and responded with missiles.

1986 Libya

U.S. air and naval forces conducted bombing strikes on terrorist facilities and military installations in Libya.

1986 Bolivia

U.S. Army personnel and aircraft assisted in antidrug operations.

1987–88 Persian Gulf

The United States increased U.S. Navy forces operating in the Persian Gulf and adopted a policy of reflagging and escorting Kuwaiti oil tankers through the gulf.

1988 Panama

The U.S. sent one thousand supplemental troops to Panama, to "further safeguard the canal, U.S. lives, property and interests in the area."

1989   Libya

Two U.S. Navy F-14 aircraft shot down two Libyan jet fighters over the Mediterranean Sea.

Administration of George Bush · January 1989–January 1993

1989   Panama

A brigade-sized force of approximately one thousand nine hundred troops was sent to augment the estimated eleven thousand U.S. forces already in the area.

1989   Andean Initiative in War on Drugs

Military and law enforcement assistance began to Colombia, Bolivia, and Peru to help them combat illicit drug producers and traffickers.

1989   Philippines

U.S. fighter planes assisted the Aquino government in repelling a coup attempt. Marines were sent to protect the U.S. embassy.

1989   Panama

U.S. military forces were ordered into Panama to protect the lives of American citizens and bring General Noriega to justice.

1990   Liberia

A reinforced rifle company was sent to provide additional security to the U.S. embassy, and helicopter teams evacuated U.S. citizens.

1990   Persian Gulf

Substantial elements of the U.S. armed forces were deployed into the region to help defend Saudi Arabia after the invasion of Kuwait by Iraq.

1991 Persian Gulf

U.S. armed forces commenced combat operations against Iraqi forces and military targets in Iraq and Kuwait.

1991 Zaire

U.S. forces transported Belgian troops and equipment into the country.

1992 Sierra Leone

U.S. forces evacuated all nonessential U.S. government workers and families.

1992 Former Yugoslavia

The U.S. participated in airlifts into Sarajevo and naval monitoring of United Nations sanctions.

1992 Somalia

U.S. forces landed to protect relief convoys in the war-torn country.

1993 Iraq

U.S. forces bombed military targets in and around Baghdad after Iraqi violation of the cease-fire.

This list, based on studies of the Congressional Research Service of the Library of Congress, includes instances when the United States used its armed forces in situations of conflict or potential conflict or for other than normal peacetime purposes.

Panama in the 1980s. Most recently, in 1991, America was the driving power in the Persian Gulf War against Iraq. In some cases, our armed forces were defending territories from aggression; in others, we initiated military action ourselves.

Many Americans have disagreed strongly on whether we

should have been involved in most of the post–World War II conflicts. Doubtful purposes, high casualty rates, and lack of rapid military success can arouse intense opposition to military action. It is important to remember how powerful an impact young people can have on the policies of our nation. We have already noted how tens of thousands of students helped to end racial discrimination with their lunch counter sit-ins. The environmental movement was given great impetus when young Americans organized Earth Day and insisted on laws to protect the quality of our land, air, and water. During the late 1960s, many young citizens rose up in anger to demand an end to the Vietnam War, and were finally successful in convincing political leaders to bring our troops home.

My daughter, Amy, was arrested in 1986 for joining other students in demonstrating against what they considered to be illegal activities of the U.S. government in Nicaragua. They were later tried by a jury and found innocent under a Massachusetts law because their violation of the law against demonstrating was less serious than the crimes they were trying to prevent. American government aid to the Contra War in Nicaragua was never supported by more than one-third of the people in our country. In both Vietnam and Nicaragua, our leaders were attempting to conceal facts about U.S. activities in the conflicts. There is no doubt that public debates and a requirement for official declarations of war would let our citizens know the truth and thereby greatly reduce the number of conflicts in which America and other nations become involved.

Almost all American families have been touched by the tragedy of war at one point in their history, or at least have had members who served in the military during a time of national crisis. Families who have recently emigrated to America often come with experiences of war in other countries. My own father was a first lieutenant in the U.S. Army during World War I; I served in the navy during World War II and the Korean conflict; my oldest son volunteered for the military and was sent to Vietnam. It is natural that we grieve over losses among our own troops. It is not so easy to sympathize with the pain of families in other nations—particularly if their sons or husbands have fought against our forces or those of our friends or allies.

We have been very fortunate that except for the bombing of Pearl Harbor in Hawaii on the morning of December 7, 1941, Americans have not seen combat on our own soil since the Civil War and battles between U.S. troops and Native Americans in the last century. Other nations have not been so fortunate, and we will hear more about their struggles in the next chapter.

4

CONFLICT TODAY

A Snapshot of the World at War

An ever-growing proportion of the American population is too young to remember war between the major world
powers. Until the conflict in the Persian Gulf, almost an entire
generation of Americans had little direct knowledge of war
involving the United States. Many Americans tend to assume
that everyone is at peace when we and our close allies are not
at war. When a conflict arises among the nations of eastern and
western Europe, we do pay attention. The majority of Americans are closely tied by kinship to the people of these countries.
Yet when the conflict is elsewhere in the world, no matter how
serious or deadly, most of us tend to ignore it, believing it has
nothing to do with us.

The fact is that advances in technology, communication, and

transportation have linked the United States closely to more places around the globe than ever before. As the only remaining superpower, we are increasingly tied both economically and socially to all other nations in the world. Many countries look to us for leadership and guidance, as well as for financial support. Our own dependence upon other regions for natural resources and for trade is constantly increasing, and serious disputes on any continent now affect us directly. We saw evidence of this when Saddam Hussein invaded Kuwait and gasoline prices in the United States rose as much as twenty-nine cents a gallon.

One reason for the large number of wars being fought today is that there are so many more nations in the world. When the United Nations was established, there were fifty-one members; in 1993, there are one hundred seventy-eight. Civil wars are more likely to break out in these smaller, more recently independent countries. Since 1945, in fact, the vast majority of the wars that have been fought have taken place in poor nations that have not yet benefited from the wealth and stability of industrialized societies like our own. These are known as less-developed countries, or LDCs. Often these more recent wars have been linked to the formation of new nations. At the end of World War II, European countries began to withdraw from their colonies in Africa, Asia, and the Middle East. Much of these colonies' natural resources had been taken, and few of the natives had been given an opportunity to learn how to govern themselves. In the early 1950s alone, fifty new nations were born. Political and social chaos often ensued.

You may be familiar with the recent fighting in what used to be called Yugoslavia. After Soviet domination ended in eastern Europe, conflicts have erupted there and in some of the newly formed Slavic republics. Freedom thus sometimes calls ancient religious and ethnic hatreds to the surface, as independent groups begin to demand their own lands and governments.

Recently, I was in Kazakhstan, about two thousand miles east of Moscow. This new nation was formerly one of the republics of the Soviet Union and is struggling to establish its own independence and unique character. There are as many Russian as Kazakh citizens living in the country, and this presents an especially difficult problem. For many years, Moscow leaders required that both government business and almost all radio and television programs be conducted in the Russian language, forcing the steady abandonment by Kazakhs of their own language and culture. Now the political leaders, mostly Kazakhs, were insisting that the official language be theirs, and Russian be used only to communicate among different ethnic groups. This argument threatens the unity of the new country. In three other former Soviet republics, no longer tightly controlled by the Soviet government and army, similar ethnic divisions have resulted in civil wars.

At the Carter Center, we count thirty-four major wars taking place right now. You may read in other places that the world has known no "major" wars since World War II, but we prefer to count all conflicts as major in which more than one thousand lives have been lost on the battlefield. In addition to these thirty-four wars, there are more than eighty lesser conflicts, in which fewer lives have been lost but where death and destruction have occurred and where the danger of escalation is always present.

By reading the brief descriptions at the end of this chapter of the world's major conflicts, as of early 1993, you will notice that all of these are civil wars, conflicts between different groups within a single country, as opposed to those between sovereign nations. You can find a map on page 56 that will help you identify any countries you may not recognize.

One characteristic that most of these modern wars share is the damage they have inflicted upon civilian populations. Civilians have always been at risk from war. But as technological power has increased, bringing improved air strike and artillery capabilities, they have begun to suffer even more. During the wars of the 1980s, many times more civilians died than military personnel. Many of these casualties were children and elderly people. Often they perished not from bombs and bullets but from lack of food and medicine. One of the worst crimes of modern-day war occurs when critical supplies are withheld from civilians by military leaders, in the hopes that such punishment will force surrender by their enemies. When cities and villages are bombed, still more citizens suffer from lack of shelter and clean water. Other citizens are abused by their own corrupt leaders, who in wartime feel free to violate human rights laws that are normally intended to provide justice and protection.

As I write, a terrible but typical example of this kind of modern war is taking place in Sudan, a country in North Africa. Armies under a Muslim government in the capital city of Khartoum have been fighting since 1983 against military units of Christians and other non-Muslims in the southern part of the country. This is a horrible conflict in which half a million people have died, soldiers and citizens alike, but most Americans do not even know about it. Along with other people from the Carter Center's International Negotiation Network, Rosalynn and I have tried to work with the two opposing forces to bring about a cease-fire. Although we have succeeded in calling some attention to the terrible famine caused by the war, our efforts to bring peace have failed. Other people and organizations have made similar efforts, but so far none has been successful.

During one of our more recent visits to Sudan, we saw the impact of war on the Dinka tribespeople living there. The Dinkas, tall and beautiful people, depend on cattle herds for their food and livelihood. Early in the war, soldiers from armies on both sides of this conflict attacked these peaceful civilians, raided their villages and farms, and stole or killed their cattle for food or profit. This left the survivors unable to support themselves. After months of wandering through desert areas, many of those who did not die of starvation or exposure settled in camps for the homeless established by the Sudanese government outside the war zone. They are known as displaced persons. (Victims of war who are forced to move from their own land to another country are called refugees.)

Rosalynn and I visited one of the camps for displaced persons near Khartoum. It was like a new city that had grown up in the middle of a huge garbage dump. There were forty-five thousand people living there, mostly children and the elderly. They represented thirteen Dinka tribes and had divided the area so that each tribe had its own territory. We could tell the difference in tribal leadership and culture just by walking through the narrow trails between the cardboard-and-rag houses. Some areas were filthy and strewn with garbage, while in other areas the people carried the waste and trash away and kept their living space as clean and neat as possible under the circumstances.

Food and water were scarce in the camp, and in order to stay alive the people had to search through the city's waste for something to eat, use, or sell. One doctor and a few nurses worked as volunteers in a small medical clinic to treat as many of the sick as possible and to immunize the children against diseases. We talked to the tribal chiefs and to the many young people who crowded around us and found that all of them had the same major desires: to return to their farms or villages, to tend their herds, and to live in peace. But we knew the leaders of their government and the revolutionary forces were neither able nor willing to make a real effort to end the nation's torture. And these Dinkas in the camps were the lucky Sudanese—they at least were alive. In just one year before our visit, more than two hundred thousand of their fellow Sudanese citizens had died in the war.

The problems caused by major wars like those in Sudan, Somalia, Mozambique, Angola, Cambodia, Sri Lanka, and other countries are staggering, but even very small conflicts have a huge impact on local communities, as freedom, property, and lives are lost in the fighting. Even when the total number of deaths from a battle is relatively small, an entire nation's economic and political system can be destroyed by the terror and persecution that takes place. The suffering people in war-torn countries cry out for help, but most often their desperate voices are not heard in rich and distant nations enjoying the blessings of peace.

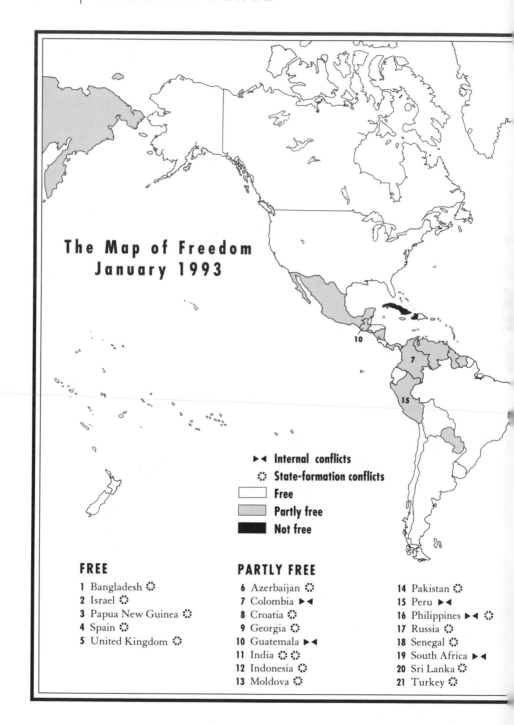

**The Map of Freedom
January 1993**

►◄ Internal conflicts
✧ State-formation conflicts
⬜ Free
◻ Partly free
⬛ Not free

FREE

1 Bangladesh ✧
2 Israel ✧
3 Papua New Guinea ✧
4 Spain ✧
5 United Kingdom ✧

PARTLY FREE

6 Azerbaijan ✧
7 Colombia ►◄
8 Croatia ✧
9 Georgia ✧
10 Guatemala ►◄
11 India ✧ ✧
12 Indonesia ✧
13 Moldova ✧

14 Pakistan ✧
15 Peru ►◄
16 Philippines ►◄ ✧
17 Russia ✧
18 Senegal ✧
19 South Africa ►◄
20 Sri Lanka ✧
21 Turkey ✧

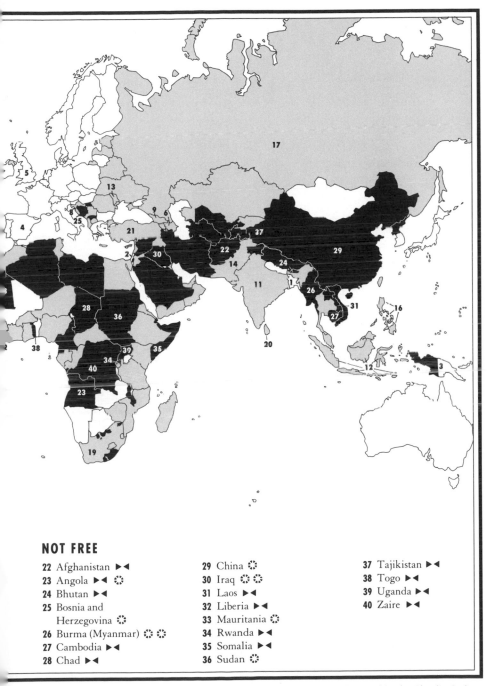

NOT FREE

22 Afghanistan ▶◀
23 Angola ▶◀ ✿
24 Bhutan ▶◀
25 Bosnia and
    Herzegovina ✿
26 Burma (Myanmar) ✿ ✿
27 Cambodia ▶◀
28 Chad ▶◀

29 China ✿
30 Iraq ✿ ✿
31 Laos ▶◀
32 Liberia ▶◀
33 Mauritania ✿
34 Rwanda ▶◀
35 Somalia ▶◀
36 Sudan ✿

37 Tajikistan ▶◀
38 Togo ▶◀
39 Uganda ▶◀
40 Zaire ▶◀

The Map of Freedom © 1993 by Freedom House. Map by Claudia Carlson.

Armed Conflicts

As of early 1993, about thirty-four major armed conflicts were under way around the world. In each of these, at least one thousand battle-related deaths had taken place. The exact numbers for 1992 and 1993 have not yet been verified by the Department of Peace and Conflict Research at Sweden's Uppsala University, which provides the official statistics of the International Negotiation Network, but the following list includes all wars likely to be considered major, as well as ten other conflicts that will probably result in fewer than one thousand deaths.

None of these conflicts began as *interstate conflicts,* wars between two internationally recognized states. They all are classified, according to the scholars at Uppsala University, either as *internal conflicts,* civil wars over the control of the government, or as *state-formation conflicts,* in which a government faces organized opposition demanding regional autonomy or independence. In several nations more than one armed conflict is taking place. In the following list, internal conflicts are indicated by a ►◄, and state-formation conflicts are indicated by a ✸.

The descriptions of the conflicts are based on a listing of ethnic conflicts that appeared in the *New York Times* on February 7, 1993. It has been revised with the advice of Professor Peter Wallensteen of Uppsala University. To find the geographic location of a particular conflict, please refer by number to the map on page 56.

EUROPE

Azerbaijan (6)

Troops from Muslim-dominated Azerbaijan, aided by Russian forces, are fighting to end a rebellion by Nagorno-Karabakh, an enclave within Azerbaijan populated largely by Christian Armenians. An estimated three thousand people on both sides have been killed since 1989, and three hundred fifty thousand Armenians and five hundred thousand Azerbaijanis have been displaced.

In addition, Kurds in western Azerbaijan are demanding autonomy and have fought Azerbaijani forces. ❖

Bosnia and Herzegovina (25)

Serbian forces have captured about 70 percent of the territory. They have carried out an "ethnic cleansing" campaign that has expelled and killed Muslims and Croats and brought widespread international condemnation. Tens of thousands of people have been estimated as killed— perhaps as many as one hundred fifty thousand killed or missing—and one and a half million uprooted from their homes. ❖

Croatia (8)

Serbian separatists control about a third of Croatia's territory. An estimated twenty-five thousand have been killed since Croatia declared independence in 1991. ❖

Georgia (9)

Abkhazia, dominated by Muslims, seeks independence or union with Russia. From seven hundred to fifteen hundred people are estimated to have been killed and eighty thousand displaced in the fighting. Southern Ossetia, also dominated by Muslims, seeks union with Northern Ossetia. About fifteen hundred are estimated to have died in the fighting. ❖

Moldova (13)

Moldova's mainly Romanian population seeks economic, political, and cultural ties with Romania. The Dniester region in eastern Moldova, where most of the population is of Russian and Ukrainian origin, declared independence in 1990, fearing that Moldova would someday unite with Romania. About eight hundred people have been killed and four thousand others have been displaced by fighting. ✸

Russia (17)

Chechenya and Ingushetia—once a single autonomous republic within the Soviet Union—have broken apart, and each seeks greater autonomy within Russia. But Ingushetia and Northern Ossetia, another region in Russia, are fighting over territory in clashes that have killed more than three hundred people. ✸

Spain (4)

Nationalists saying they represent three million Basques seek an independent state on the border of Spain and France. Since 1968, seven hundred seventeen people have been killed in Spain and forty-nine in France. ✸

United Kingdom (5)

The Protestant majority in Northern Ireland favors continued union with Britain, while the Catholic minority wants to join with the rest of Ireland. More than three thousand people have been killed in fighting between British troops, Protestant paramilitary groups, and the Irish Republican Army since 1969. ✸

MIDDLE EAST AND NORTH AFRICA

Iraq (30)

In the north, two major Kurdish parties rule in an enclave protected militarily by the United States and its allies. Several hundred have died in clashes with Iraqi forces since the 1991 Persian Gulf War. In the south, leaders of a rebellion by Shiite Muslims say that tens of thousands of Shiites have been killed by forces of the Sunni-dominated Baghdad government since the end of the Persian Gulf War. ✺ ✺

Israel (2)

The intifada, a popular uprising of Palestinians against Israeli occupation of the West Bank of the Jordan River and the Gaza Strip, erupted in 1987. About one thousand Palestinians have been killed by Israeli soldiers, five hundred have been killed by fellow Palestinians, and about one hundred Israelis have been killed in Palestinian attacks. ✺

Sudan (36)

The government, dominated by Arab Muslims from the north, is fighting a long-standing insurgency by black Christians and animists in the south. Thousands have been reported killed and millions displaced. ✺

Turkey (21)

Kurdish separatists represented by the Marxist Kurdish Workers Party have sought a separate Kurdish state in fighting that has killed twenty-five hundred since 1984. ✺

AFRICA SOUTH OF THE SAHARA

Angola (23)

Following national elections in fall 1992, renewed fighting between the government and guerrilla forces led by Jonas Savimbi, of the National Union for the Total Independence of Angola (UNITA), has left thousands dead and forced large numbers from their homes. The struggle is ideological and political in nature, with ethnic overtones. There is also a violent secessionist movement in Cabinda, an oil-producing area that is geographically separated from the rest of Angola. ▶◀ ✷

Chad (28)

President Idriss Déby, who ousted President Hissen Habré in 1990, has faced sporadic rebellions in the west and south of Chad. Some have reportedly involved clashes between Déby's Zakawa tribe and members of Habré's Gourane tribe. ▶◀

Liberia (32)

At least twenty thousand have been killed and hundreds of thousands have been uprooted in a civil war. Drawing support from the Gio and Mano ethnic groups, the guerrilla leader Charles Taylor controls most of the country. President Samuel K. Doe, from the Krahn ethnic group, was killed in 1990, and the capital city of Monrovia is held by an interim government installed by West African nations as part of a regional peace effort. ▶◀

Mauritania (33)

Government security forces under the Arab-dominated regime have clashed with opposition groups angry over expulsions and oppression of the black minority. ✷

Rwanda (34)

Fighting continues between the government, dominated by Hutu tribes, and an invading force led by the minority Tutsi tribe, despite an agreement between the government and the rebels in July 1992. Tens of thousands have died in ethnic fighting in the last thirty years. ▶◀

Senegal (18)

In Casamance, a southern region mostly populated by the Diola tribe, there is opposition to Muslim domination in the government. Hundreds have been killed and thousands have been displaced in clashes with government forces. ○

Somalia (35)

Clan fighting escalated into full-scale civil war in which three hundred thousand have died and a million made homeless from war or starvation. An American-led UN military force has intervened and tried to establish stability. ▶◀

South Africa (19)

Since 1984, about fifteen thousand have been killed in political violence related to a black insurrection against the white South African government. About three thousand were killed in 1992, many in clashes between Zulus and rival black groups. ▶◀

Togo (38)

Scores were killed last year as government forces loyal to Togo's leader, Gen. Gnassingbé Eyadéma, of the Kabiye tribe, battled opposition forces, including those from the rival Ewe tribe. ▶◀

Uganda (39)

The army, under President Yoweri K. Museveni, composed princi-
pally of members of the Baganda and Banyarwanda tribes, continues
to wage sporadic warfare with northern rebels, mainly from the
Acholi and Langi tribes. ▶◀

Zaire (40)

Thousands have died recently in the civil war between forces opposing
and loyal to President Mobutu Sese Seko. The fighting has ethnic
overtones because various forces are from competing ethnic groups
or tribes. ▶◀

ASIA

Afghanistan (22)

After the 1992 withdrawal of Soviet troops and the overthrow of the
Soviet-installed leader, Najibullah, the country has collapsed into civil
war among competing ethnic factions. The Hazars control central
and western areas near Iran, the Pathans are largely in control in the
east, and the Tajiks largely control the north. Thousands are estimated
to have been killed in recent fighting, and millions of Afghans remain
in refugee camps in Pakistan and in Iran. ▶◀

Bangladesh (1)

A migration by members of the country's Muslim majority into the
thinly populated Chittagong Hill Tracts region in the south has led
to an insurgency by the area's Chakmas, a mainly Buddhist people,
leaving hundreds dead and tens of thousands displaced. ✥

Bhutan (24)

A revolt by ethnic Nepalese against the government and reprisals by government forces have led to thousands of Nepalese fleeing the country in the last two years. ▸◂

Burma (Myanmar) (26)

In the last two years, more than two hundred fifty thousand Muslims, charging harassment, have fled across the western border to Bangladesh. Hundreds are also believed to have died in clashes between Burmese soldiers and separatist Karen and other rebels along the Thai-Burmese border in the last two years. ❂ ❂

Cambodia (27)

Rebel factions signed a peace accord ending a thirteen-year civil war. A Supreme National Council made up of the rebel factions and the Cambodian government is to advise the United Nations, which administers the country's affairs, until a new government can be formed after elections this year. Various sides are constantly threatening to walk away from the agreement.

Khmer Rouge soldiers, who blame Vietnam for many of Cambodia's problems, have been carrying out attacks on the one hundred thousand Vietnamese living in Cambodia. ▸◂

China (29)

Tibetans rebelled against Chinese rule in 1959, with an estimated eighty-seven thousand Tibetans killed. After a relaxation of Chinese rule, Beijing cracked down again in 1987. Several dozen people are believed to have been killed in various incidents. In Xinjiang, China suppressed a rebellion among Muslims of Turkic descent in 1990, and an estimated fifty people died. ❖

India (11)

Tensions between Hindus and Muslims exploded when Hindu militants razed a mosque in the northern state of Uttar Pradesh. Rioting that followed in many places across India led to two thousand killings by official count, and many more by unofficial estimates. Killings by Muslims and Hindus continue. In Kashmir, five thousand militants, civilians, and Indian troops have been killed since a rebellion by the largely Muslim population began in 1990. An estimated one hundred twenty thousand people, mostly Hindus, have fled Kashmir for other parts of India.

In Punjab, about twenty thousand Hindus and Sikhs are estimated to have been killed since a rebellion by Sikh militants erupted in 1982. In Assam, more than two hundred have been reported killed since an insurgency by secessionists erupted in 1990. In Nagaland, insurgent Bodos have been fighting for a separate state; about three hundred people have been killed. ❖ ❖

Indonesia (12)

A civil war broke out in East Timor in 1975 after Portugal withdrew from its former colony, and Indonesia crushed the pro-independence rebellion. Human rights groups charge that one hundred thousand to two hundred thousand of the six hundred thousand mostly Roman Catholic East Timorese have died of starvation, disease, or execution since Indonesia annexed the area.

A separatist movement also exists in northern Sumatra, where Indonesian forces are said by Amnesty International to have killed two thousand. ❖

Laos (31)

Sporadic attacks by Hmong insurgents are intended to destabilize the Communist government that took power in 1975. ▶◀

Pakistan (14)

Thousands have died in conflicts between government forces and groups of secessionists and dissidents in Sindh and the Northwest Frontier Province. There has also been rioting in Karachi involving descendants of Muslims who emigrated from India at the time of partition with Pakistan in 1947. ⚙

Papua New Guinea (3)

Rebels on the island of Bougainville declared independence in 1990. The Papua New Guinea government subdued the rebellion in 1991. ⚙

Philippines (16)

The New People's Army, a group affiliated with the Communist party, continues a long-term effort to seize power. The government is also fighting the Mindanao National Liberation Front and the Moro Islamic Liberation Front, independence movements on the island of Mindanao. ▶◀ ⚙

Sri Lanka (20)

An insurgency by mostly Hindu Tamils in the north and east has been carried out against the government, which is dominated by the mostly Buddhist Sinhalese. Since 1983, an estimated twenty-eight thousand people have been killed in the Tamil rebellion, and another fifty thousand in the government's crackdown on Sinhalese militants. ⚙

Tajikistan (37)

Tens of thousands of Tajik Muslims have been driven from their land by resurgent Communist armies seeking to suppress Islamic political power. More than twenty-five thousand have been killed and five hundred thousand displaced since 1991. ▸◂

LATIN AMERICA

Colombia (7)

A group representing rights of Indians, Quintin Lamee, suspended an armed rebellion in 1991, but other Marxist groups claiming to represent peasants are continuing guerrilla attacks on the government. ▸◂

Guatemala (10)

An essentially political conflict between the Guatemalan government and leftist guerrillas has had ethnic overtones because of the long history of repression of Indians in Guatemala. At least forty-three thousand Guatemalan refugees have fled into Mexico, but some are beginning to return. ▸◂

Peru (15)

Since 1980, a Maoist guerrilla group known as Shining Path has waged war and won control of about a third of Peruvian territory. Shining Path draws support from the largely Indian or mixed-race populations that are resisting the control of the mostly Hispanic elite in Lima. About twenty-six thousand people have been killed in the war, and an estimated six hundred thousand have fled their homes to other parts of the country. Thousands more have emigrated. ▸◂

© 1993 by The New York Times Company. Reprinted by permission.

5

FOOD, SHELTER, AND HEALTH CARE

The Foundations of Peace

Nutritious food, safe shelter, and good health are our three most important physical needs. Yet hundreds of millions of people around the globe exist from day to day with very poor diets, sometimes receiving almost no nourishment at all. Many also must learn how to survive for long periods of time without any housing or medical care. This is true even in America, the wealthiest nation in the world. Forced to provide for themselves and their children as best they can, these people are fighting their own kind of war.

Often the war against poverty and deprivation coincides with military combat. In pitched battle, soldiers may damage, raid, or destroy food sources and shelter, leaving the most dependent civilians—the young, the old, and the poor—even more vulnerable. Public sanitation and personal hygiene become difficult among the masses of gathered refugees and displaced persons, causing diseases to spread quickly. Injuries suffered during the fighting, or by the resulting destruction, burden even the most expert health care providers. When mothers and fathers are killed, children are often left without anyone to take care of them. In this chapter, we're going to talk about what can be done to make the three basic building blocks of peace—food, shelter, and health care—available to everyone, in times of both peace and war.

FOOD

Without a doubt, the world's worst hunger problems can be found in the African countries below the Sahara Desert. Fully one-fourth of the people who live in this vast area do not get enough to eat. This problem gets worse every day, as the population increases more rapidly than the production of food. The average person in less-developed countries eats one thousand fewer calories a day than the average person in western Europe or America.

The startling truth about this severe food shortage is that there is actually not a lack of food. There is only a lack of food *in some places*. Worldwide, more food is produced each year than the human population can eat, and this adequate total food supply is likely to continue. Moreover, agricultural specialists have researched technology that could further improve food production, storage, and transportation. Through genetic engineering, scientists are discovering how to improve the hardiness and nutritive value of certain crops. The Carter Center has a special program in Africa to introduce a new, highly nutritious white corn that contains two vital food ingredients all corn has previously lacked. Yet these technological gains mean nothing if food does not reach those people who continue to suffer from famine.

In the African country of Ghana and other less-developed countries, farming families do not own their own farms. Their governments or local chiefs own the land, permitting the farmers to work only a few acres each year for themselves. Official regulations in many of these countries are often designed to keep food prices low, a policy that benefits the politically powerful city-dwelling consumers at the expense of the farmers. When the farmers no longer make a profit from their crops, they lose their incentive to harvest more grain than they themselves need.

The ancient traditional farming practices employed in these regions also contribute to low yields. Some farmers in Ghana, for instance, use a technique called slash-and-burn. Each year, when they prepare to plant corn, sorghum, or millet, the farmers cut trees and burn bushes and grass to clear a plot. They plant the seeds randomly about the field in open spots between the dead bushes and tree stumps, adding no fertilizer. After one or two crops grow this way, the soil is depleted of nutrients and the farmers slash-and-burn a new patch of forest. The Carter Center, through a program called Global 2000, encourages the native farmers to stop this costly practice, teaching them how to grow more plants of the best species in regular, curved rows that prevent erosion and to add enough fertilizer. This not only protects the land and trees but also saves the farmers an enormous amount of labor each year in preparing fields for planting.

In the early 1980s, famine caused by land depletion and other reasons, including war and drought, ravaged twenty-two African countries. The world spotlight was turned to the problem of chronic hunger, and a number of international organizations got involved to help the countries recover and to try to prevent future starvation. In 1986, Global 2000 and the Sasakawa Africa Association, a Japanese philanthropic group, formed a partnership under the guidance of Dr. Norman Borlaug, a famous agricultural specialist. Dr. Borlaug helped to bring a "green revolution" to India and Pakistan in the early 1970s by dramatically increasing their production of rice and other food grains. Millions of starving people in these two countries were then able to obtain more food from their own fields. He received the Nobel Peace Prize for this accomplishment. Our goal is to bring the same benefits to some of the African countries that have been afflicted with famine and starvation. Dr. Borlaug and I visited Tanzania, Ghana, Zambia, and Sudan in 1986 and began a grass-roots movement among small farmers so that they could begin to help themselves out of the vicious cycle of crop failure and famine. Our program has continued successfully since that time, growing each year.

Each nation's government agreed to guarantee fair market prices and to provide agricultural workers who could join our small staff in helping to increase crop yields. Since then, our food production projects have been extended to include Benin, Togo, Nigeria, and Ethiopia. In cooperation with their own governments, we have helped to arrange enough financial credit to farm families so that they can buy fertilizer and good seed. They have been able to repay these loans easily from a portion of their increased yields. We do not encourage the use of costly, difficult-to-maintain equipment like tractors. In fact, in only a few cases have farmers bought oxen to help with the planting. Most of the work is done with hoes and other hand tools. If harvested crops can be stored for several months before being sold, farmers have the power to wait for the right price in the marketplace, so we also encouraged the development of better crop storage methods. The Food and Agriculture Organization of the United Nations has worked with us on ways to protect the harvested crops from insects, rodents, and spoilage.

The Global 2000 program begins in a few dozen villages on a small scale, with perhaps one farmer in each community who is willing to demonstrate new growing techniques. These test farmers agree to grow about half their acreage in what are called production test plots, side by side with a similar plot using traditional methods. In this way, as the crop flourishes, the comparison on each farm between the two plots can be observed by the whole community. Word spreads, and the program grows by leaps and bounds. In Sudan, I have seen hundreds of farmers walk long distances to learn about the new farming methods. In Ghana, we began with only forty farmers in 1986. Average yields almost tripled. By the next year, there were twelve hundred farmers, and in 1988, sixteen thousand families joined our program. Soon five times this many of their neighbors were participating, benefiting from higher yields as well. In fact, we made a mistake by increasing production too rapidly. There was not enough grain storage on farms or in villages, and the markets were flooded with surplus corn. The price dropped far below the cost of production, and farmers were not able to sell their crops and repay their small loans. After this unfortunate experience, we have been more careful to match storage facilities with the size of the grain harvest. We also now limit the number of farm families in our program to fewer than twenty thousand and bring in new farmers only as others, knowing how to maintain high yields, "graduate" after two or three years.

Once the program gets going in a region, we try to shift the responsibility for it from our workers to local officials and other organizations. The farmers themselves often improve upon what they have learned and share that knowledge with others. Last year in Tanzania, near Mount Kilimanjaro, we visited a community where the farm families had combined their acreage to plant large fields. By banding together, they were able to use oxen and simple machinery, buy fertilizer and seed at lower prices, and get more money for their surplus grain at harvest time or when the market was strongest. They even employed their own trained agricultural advisers.

When I travel to Africa and see the test farms for myself, much more productive than before, I am happy for the program's success. But severe problems remain in Africa. Millions of farm families do not take advantage of improved agricultural practices, and government policies hinder production and distribution of food grain. Even when food is made available in the market, many people remain hungry because they are too poor to buy it at any price. Hunger also makes them more susceptible to illness and less able to work productively toward improving their economic state. In most countries in the developing world, families spend more than half their income on food. In the very poorest places, some must spend as much as 90 percent, even when the food for sale is not adequate for a proper diet.

Another remaining problem in Africa is the scarcity and high cost of transportation. When trains, trucks, and boats are not available to deliver seed and fertilizer or to ship vegetables and grains, production suffers, food is wasted, and lives can be lost. With other organizations, we work on some aspects of this problem, too. One important step in tackling the question of food distribution is smoothing the way for cooperation between different countries in the same area. Nations torn apart by strife or war cannot usually participate in partnerships to feed their citizens.

In civil wars, typically transportation is interrupted, crops destroyed, and farmers and villagers driven from their homes. Thousands of homeless people attempt to move to urban areas, where they hope to obtain food, shelter, and medical care. Many of them either die on the journey or perish in the overcrowded cities, where few supplies exist. In Somalia, for example, from 1988 to early 1991 a bloody civil war reigned. This resulted in a deadly famine that by 1992 had already claimed hundreds of thousands of lives, and nearly one and a half million people still face the threat of starvation.

Guerrilla bands have been on the rampage in Somalia since 1978. This was a special disaster because the president of the country, Mohammed Siyad Barre, and his family were ruthless oppressors of their own citizens. Many ethnic groups organized local armies to defend themselves, and their commanders, known by the media as warlords, later began to fight one another for land and power. Anarchy resulted, with no central government in charge of the nation's affairs. When the outside world finally became aware of the suffering of the Somalians and sent food and medicine for relief, the warlords simply stole the supplies for their own troops or for resale at exorbitant prices.

Respect for human life disappeared. International troops were sent to Somalia by the United Nations in 1992 and succeeded in helping to deliver food to many of the starving people. Unless some form of democratic government can be formed in the country, however, it is likely that the warlords will just wait to resume their criminal activities after the foreign troops leave Somalia.

In addition to preventing or ending wars like this one before they can take such a devastating toll, we need to help the world food supply reach all of the world's people. Governments, international organizations, universities, agricultural businesses, and private citizens must join together in helping a "green revolution" come to Africa.

SHELTER

As much as we may not like to admit it, there are many malnourished people in our country, despite the enormous surplus of food produced on American farms and ranches. Another, often related social problem has grown so serious that few Americans can ignore it: homelessness.

In the richest American cities, people without homes can be seen living on the streets and standing in line for food at soup kitchens or for beds in temporary shelters. It is estimated that there are sixty thousand homeless people in New York City, twelve thousand in Atlanta, and like numbers in other metropolitan areas. Thousands of other people live in substandard private shelters and government housing developments. The numbers increase each year, with more and more women and children among those without decent dwellings. An average of one hundred thousand children in America sleep on the streets or in temporary shelters every single night.

One of the main problems that homeless people face is stigma, which literally means a mark or brand of shame. Some more privileged members of society label the homeless on sight as unworthy, lazy, or even worse—as drug users and thieves. While it is true that some homeless people are lazy, and others are addicted to drugs and alcohol, many have only lost their jobs and are unable to afford a place to live. Some of them are parents with small children. And still others are mentally ill, which carries an additional stigma. New York City estimates that fully one-third of its homeless people are severely mentally ill. Our wealthy society should realize that a decent place to live is a basic human right for all its citizens, especially for those who are unable to care for themselves.

Rosalynn and I enjoy working one week a year for an organization called Habitat for Humanity. Habitat was started by Millard and Linda Fuller in 1976. Millard had made a lot of money as an attorney, but he and his wife became disillusioned with their extravagant and busy life-style. They donated all their money to charity and began to build houses for homeless people, first on a farm near our home in Plains, Georgia, and then in Zaire, in central Africa. Fifteen years ago, they started to organize local Habitat groups throughout the United States and in other nations around the world.

The purpose of Habitat for Humanity is to work side by side with indigent people to build or renovate homes. This construction is meant to supplement the other housing that private and government organizations are already building. No state or federal funds are accepted by the program, and it is not based on charity. Instead, the prospective homeowners are required to work for hundreds of hours on their own house and on those of their neighbors. When the house is completed, it is theirs, but they also have to pay back the building costs over a period of about twenty years. Habitat does not make any kind of profit for itself, nor does it charge interest on the loan for the building costs, practicing the economics of the Bible: "If you lend money to my people, to the poor among you, you shall not deal with them as a creditor; you shall not exact interest from them" (Exodus 22:25).

Careful management and the use of volunteer labor mean that the price of the home will not be beyond the family's ability to pay. In Nicaragua, workers even make their own bricks and roof tiles from local clay to keep expenses down. On the average, it costs about ten times as much money in United States dollars to build a house in the United States as it does in a developing nation.

The work of building a house requires many skills. One of our new homeowners in New York City was later accepted as an apprentice by the local carpenter's union because of what she learned on the job while building her Habitat home. The best reward of all is watching the joy and restored dignity of those who receive the homes—knowing that their own work has made it possible. Few people are really looking for charity. Instead, they just seek the opportunity to work for a better life.

War and homelessness are closely interrelated. In many civil conflicts, hundreds of thousands of people have their homes destroyed or are forced to flee from the fighting. I have visited Liberia several times. When the civil war erupted in this nation, more than half the total population were driven from their home communities, and a majority of these people were actually forced to cross the borders into neighboring countries, becoming refugees. Also, some conflicts begin when people without shelter or other basic human rights seek better lives for themselves and their families by taking up weapons to fight against their own government or their neighbors.

HEALTH CARE

When I was a boy, growing up in Georgia, a major illness in one family was considered a serious event by the whole community. Many people would go to the home of a person who was ill, offering food and support. They would maintain a day-and-night vigil in the parlor and front yard, hoping for good news. This was before miracle drugs and during the Great Depression, when people could not afford hospital care.

When my mother nursed the people who lived around us in our rural community near Plains, they sometimes were unable to pay her the thirty-five cents an hour that nurses were supposed to receive. Instead, they brought her eggs, a chicken or two, blackberries, or something else she could use. Once for several weeks she nursed a little girl who had a kind of anemia. When the girl died, her father was doubly distressed because he could not pay my mother. A few weeks later, he brought us a wagonload of turpentine chips, which burst into flame when they got close to a lit match. We used them for years to start fires in our cookstove and fireplaces.

In those early days, when there was a threat to community health, everyone immediately responded. I remember that every child in town would line up for shots to prevent typhoid, typhus,

In a cubicle off a third-floor ward, a short walk from the center island where amputees' beds had been wheeled as protection from the Serbian gun positions in the mountains, Dr. Mufid Lazovic sat with his head in his hands. In passionate, often overwrought bursts, he talked of his bitter experiences working as a surgeon on legions of people wounded in the siege.

"For the first time in my career, I come in fear to work," he said. "I never know what awaits me, but I am always sure of one thing, that I cannot give the patients the help they need. It is a terrible thing to have to live with, to know that if we had the equipment and the power and the materials, we could be doing so

and other diseases. On "dog inoculation day," all the town veterinarians would vaccinate pets against rabies. With the crowds waiting in line, it was almost like a holiday, and I would sell three times as many of my boiled peanuts as usual. (Selling peanuts was my summer job.)

Today most neighborhoods no longer have the same attitude toward community health, in part because the study of medicine has made so much progress. My favorite aunt in Plains died of strep throat, an illness that is now easily treated at home with simple antibiotics from the pharmacy. Many diseases that were prevalent among Americans fifty years ago are now much less common, including polio, tetanus, typhus, typhoid fever, hookworm, diphtheria, and pneumonia. One, smallpox, has even been eliminated worldwide. But, whether or not we are aware of a community spirit, we all still fight together against invisible public enemies: AIDS and other viruses, cancer, heart disease, much more. And there is always the question: What have these people done to deserve this? What have they ever done to earn so much hatred?"

The lack of electricity means that often surgeons must work with no power other than that supplied by an emergency battery, an army unit that sits in a box on the operating-room floor. This powers a single light, and some but not all of the anesthesiology equipment. More than two hundred operations, some of them to remove deeply lodged bullets and mortar fragments or infected tissue, have been conducted without X rays or respiratory monitors.

JOHN F. BURNS
New York Times *reporter, in Sarajevo*

alcoholism. In the United States, there is still much work to be done in providing good pre and postnatal care for mothers and infants, immunizations for preschoolers, and good health care for older people.

Unfortunately, the medical advances Americans can take for granted have not reached many people in other nations, some of whom still die from diseases we barely remember. The Task Force for Child Survival and Development at the Carter Center has the major responsibility of helping the World Health Organization, UNICEF (the UN organization that specializes in child welfare), the United Nations Development Program, and other groups work as a team as they strive to immunize children against polio, measles, tetanus, diphtheria, and whooping cough and to treat diarrhea. In a period of just five years, beginning in 1985, the percentage of immunized children in developing nations jumped from 20 percent to 80 percent.

The task force headquarters is located at the Carter Center, but the thousands of health workers who carry out its programs live all over the world. On one occasion, I was asked to help with an immunization program in Colombia. It was a massive nationwide effort. The president of the country had marshaled the news media, police, schoolteachers, parents, religious leaders, and other people throughout the country to bring all the children to central locations to be vaccinated. Shortly before the scheduled time, a volcano erupted. More than twenty thousand people were buried under an enormous wave of lava and mud. As I went from village to village near the volcano, I witnessed the dedication of the Colombian people to the health of their children as they struggled to keep the vaccination schedule. Another example of such dedication occurred during a terrible war in El Salvador, when both government and revolutionary leaders agreed to hold a three-day cease-fire each year to carry out an immunization program.

In spite of this good progress, about fifteen million children still die each year from diseases that could easily be prevented or cured with the medicines and technology we currently possess. Believe it or not, diarrhea kills more children than almost any other disease worldwide—thousands of boys and girls a day—although it can be cured with a basic mixture of sugar and salt dissolved in water. Health workers in developing nations are teaching mothers and midwives how to rehydrate infants and children who have diarrhea with this solution so they do not perish. An even better way to stop this terrible tragedy would be to prevent it in the first place. Children must be guaranteed access to clean water, sanitary toilets, and fresh food.

The biggest risk factor worldwide among adults, causing or contributing to over two and a half million deaths a year, is also preventable: cigarette smoking. As well-educated people in America learn of the deadly nature of smoking and give up the habit, American tobacco companies are increasing their advertisement of cigarettes in poorer U.S. neighborhoods and in foreign nations to make up for the lost buyers. If nothing is done to stop this criminal effort, cigarettes may kill as many as ten million people a year by the end of this century.

The idea of tackling a specific disease and removing it from the face of the planet is daunting. But it has been done once with smallpox, and health care workers intend to do it again. Through the Task Force on Disease Eradication, also located at the Carter Center, two diseases have been targeted for eradication by the end of this century: polio and guinea worm.

Concentrated efforts have been mounted against polio for many years, long before the Carter Center was established. Health specialists are convinced that the last case of the disease has been seen in North and South America and the Caribbean. By the end of the century, we hope polio can be conquered in Africa and Asia as well.

The guinea worm is a particularly horrible parasite that still contaminates drinking water in India and in sixteen countries in Africa. Five million people of all ages are afflicted with the disease every year. They drink water that contains the eggs, which develop inside the body for about a year, growing into worms more than two feet long. The mature worms then penetrate the skin and slowly emerge through large sores over a period of several weeks. When the parasites emerge near a child's

Sample Questions
from the Health Risk Appraisal

1. Sex: *Male   Female*
2. Age:
3. Height:
4. Weight:
5. Body Frame Size: *Small   Medium   Large*
6. What is your blood pressure?
7. What is your TOTAL cholesterol?
8. How would you describe your cigarette smoking habit?
   Never smoke—go to question 12
   Used to smoke—go to question 10
   Still smoke—go to question 9
9. How many cigarettes a day do you smoke?
10. How many years has it been since you smoked regularly?
11. What was the average number of cigarettes a day you smoked then?
12. In the next 12 months, how many miles will you travel by car, truck, or van? By motorcycle?
13. On a typical day, how do you usually travel?
walk	*midsize or full-size car*
bicycle	*truck or van*
motorcycle	*bus, subway, or train*
subcompact or compact car	*mostly stay home*
14. What percentage of the time do you buckle your seat belt?
15. On the average, how close to the speed limit do you drive?
16. How many times in the last month did you drive or ride when the driver had too much alcohol to drink?
17. How many alcoholic drinks do you have in a typical week?

Women (Questions 18–22)

18. At what age did you have your first menstrual period?
19. How old were you when your first child was born?
20. How many women in your natural family have had breast cancer?
21. How long has it been since you have had a Pap smear test?
22. How often do you examine your breasts for lumps?

Men (Question 23)

23. How long has it been since you have had a rectal or prostate exam?

24. How many times in the last year did you witness or become involved in a violent fight or attack where there was a good chance of serious injury to someone?
25. In an average week, how many times do you engage in physical activity (exercise or work that lasts at least 20 minutes without stopping and which is hard enough to make you breathe heavier and your heart beat faster)?
26. Do you eat some food every day that is high in fiber, such as whole-grain bread, cereal, fresh fruits or vegetables?
27. Have you suffered a personal loss or misfortune in the past year that has had a serious impact on your life?
28. In general, how satisfied are you with your life?

knee or other joint, they may cripple the victim permanently, almost like polio. People have learned the hard way that it is best not to pull on the worms as they emerge. If the worm breaks, it will die inside the skin and may cause very serious, even fatal, infection. Suffering from guinea worm disease, millions of people miss months of school and work, wasted time which has a serious impact on the whole population.

Guinea worm can be prevented by avoiding contaminated water. In some countries, water accumulates in reservoirs during the rainy season and is used for drinking and cooking. This water is often stagnant and polluted. In a few fortunate villages, deep wells are being dug to provide clean water. In other villages, people have learned that water can be boiled before drinking to sterilize it, but this is too time-consuming and requires scarce fuel wood for the fire. An American manufacturing company has donated millions of special filters so that water can be strained. Another company has donated a chemical that can be added to ponds to kill guinea worm eggs but still leave the water safe to drink. Thanks to an extraordinary effort of international compassion and cooperation, this story can have a happy ending: The disease should be completely eradicated by 1996.

Having the knowledge to eliminate a disease like guinea worm and applying that knowledge are two different things. This is as true in the United States as in less-developed countries. In 1986, the Carter Center conducted a program called Closing the Gap, meaning the gap between what we know about preventing sickness and death and what we choose to do about it. Out of this study came the Health Risk Appraisal (HRA), which helps people analyze their own health habits. Based on this information, the HRA then explains, confidentially, what health habits a person can change to add years to his or her life. An excellent time to take such an appraisal is in high school. Even before you enter college or the working world, you will begin to make more choices about your life-style than at any other time.

Many of the health problems of today are driven by personal behavior. The choices we make on a day-to-day basis largely determine whether we will take abusive substances, become unwilling parents, acquire a sexually transmitted disease, or suffer a violent injury. When the Carter Center developed the HRA, some interesting facts came to light. It turns out that over two-thirds of all illnesses and premature deaths that occur before the age of sixty-five are preventable, just by modifying personal habits concerning diet, exercise, sexual encounters, the use of firearms, and drugs. Cigarettes have become the foremost preventable cause of death in our country, costing the lives of more than four hundred thousand Americans each year. We are all ultimately responsible for our own good health.

6

PROTECTING THE ENVIRONMENT

The Earth, Our Home

We talk a lot about the environment these days. We celebrate Earth Day each spring, buy "green" books, recycle bottles and newspapers, and study ecology in science classes. But what does all this have to do with peacemaking?

Like food, shelter, and health care, the environment can be considered a vital human resource. It should be protected from the ravages of war. In times of peace, the environment should be shared and used wisely.

Although it is perhaps more obvious why good food and housing are essential to our standard of living, we actually depend on the environment in the most fundamental way of all. The life that surrounds us in the oceans, in the air, and on land provides the raw materials for our survival. All living things are interconnected in a web of cooperation. When human actions disrupt the patterns of the natural world, the conflict that results endangers the future of entire species—including our own.

Miraculous in its complexity and beauty, the environment can be permanently damaged. Human technology now has the power to alter the landscape of the entire earth and its support systems. What are some of the major problems confronting the environment today?

OZONE DEPLETION

We have damaged an upper part of the earth's atmosphere called the ozone layer by releasing into the air harmful chlorofluorocarbons (CFCs), industrial chemicals used primarily in refrigeration and aerosol cans. The ozone layer is a critical natural shield that protects our delicate human skin and eyes from the burning ultraviolet rays of the sun. If ozone depletion continues, human cancer deaths may increase dramatically. The ability of plants to survive and grow is also harmed by changes in radiation from the sun. Some plankton and other small aquatic organisms, which support the oceans' food chain, die when exposed to even small increases in ultraviolet radiation.

DEFORESTATION

During the past ten thousand years, about one-third of the earth's forest cover has disappeared, mostly in the industrialized nations. For instance, in the United States, only 15 percent of our original forests survive, mostly in Alaska. Especially during the last ten years, our government has been selling these virgin trees rapidly. In Europe practically no original forests still exist.

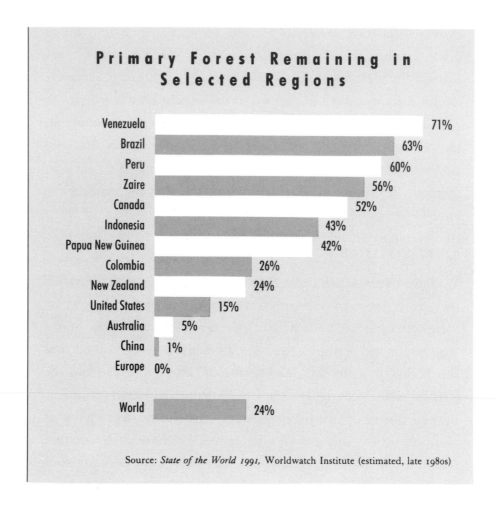

Primary Forest Remaining in Selected Regions

Region	Percent
Venezuela	71%
Brazil	63%
Peru	60%
Zaire	56%
Canada	52%
Indonesia	43%
Papua New Guinea	42%
Colombia	26%
New Zealand	24%
United States	15%
Australia	5%
China	1%
Europe	0%
World	24%

Source: *State of the World 1991*, Worldwatch Institute (estimated, late 1980s)

We severely criticize countries like Brazil, where 63 percent of their forests remain, and Indonesia, where 43 percent survive. For the entire world, about 1 percent of primary forests are being harvested every year.

Some developing countries, however, have harvested and exported almost all their trees. I have flown over such areas in Africa and the Caribbean and observed the result of these unwise practices. One can easily see the border between Liberia, where forests still stand, and Côte d'Ivoire, where they are gone. The same devastating comparison can be made when traveling from the Dominican Republic into Haiti. In the Queen Charlotte Islands, on the west coast of Canada, I have watched while loggers with especially long chain saws cut every tree on the steep mountainsides, some of which were giants, more than six feet in diameter. The Canadian forest areas will likely be re-seeded, but so far there is no global program to encourage poorer nations to reforest their land.

There is a special concern about tropical rain forests, which are the most complex, diverse ecosystems on earth, home to millions of species of plants and animals as well as hundreds of thousands of humans. Originally situated in three big blocks near the equator, in Africa, South America, and Southeast Asia, the rain forests are under threat from overharvesting of trees for sale and for use as fuel and from slashing-and-burning to permit farming and ranching. Only about half of them remain, and they are still disappearing quickly. If these natural treasures are lost, valuable birds, animals, fruits, oils, spices, nuts, medicines, and many other rain forest products will be lost with them.

In satellite photographs, many regions of the world that used to be a lush green are now a dry brown. One of the causes of this drought is deforestation. When the world's forests are cut, the local climate is disturbed. An entire region can become drier. The soil becomes infertile, deserts advance, and human populations, no longer able to grow crops, become displaced.

Deforestation also harms rivers and streams. As trees are cut extensively, the soil washes away, polluting streams and nearby oceans and fish and other aquatic populations. Since fish are a main source of food for people who live in dense forests and along seacoasts, where farming is marginal, this is another way that environmental damage harms humans.

GLOBAL WARMING

Carbon dioxide (CO_2), methane, and other gases emitted from industry and from the burning of forests and grasslands are being trapped in the earth's atmosphere. These gases allow sunlight to penetrate to the earth's surface, but they prevent the heat that radiates back from escaping into space. This means that the earth may be warming substantially. Some scientists believe that this global warming is already affecting temperature and rainfall patterns enough to reduce crop yields and speed up the formation of deserts. Extensive studies of temperature readings over the past years seem to support this theory. If global warming does continue, continental glaciers and the polar ice caps may melt. Ocean levels will rise, eventually flooding vital coastal areas, threatening homes and crops and affecting the quality of groundwater supplies. It is important to note that forests are crucial "CO_2 sinks." About 20 percent of the world's supply of this gas is absorbed by trees and replaced with oxygen.

LOSS OF BIODIVERSITY

One of the most urgent environmental problems is the loss of diversity. *Biodiversity* is the term used to describe the richness of life that has evolved on our planet. Humans and other animals depend on this wide variety of creatures and plants for their very existence. When species become extinct, we are limiting the ability of future generations to survive.

Plants and animals are less able to protect themselves from

blight, disease, and changes in climate when their natural habitats are harmed. And when rain forests or other special habitats are destroyed completely, the earth loses an unknown number of insects, plants, and animals that lived only in those regions and in no others. Once a species is extinct, it cannot be re-created, even in a laboratory. The destruction of one species may also harm many others that are dependent upon it. Unique and irreplaceable stores of genetic information thus are lost each time a species disappears. Its potential benefit to scientific knowledge or medicine is gone forever.

OVERPOPULATION

Another way in which humans have fundamentally altered the balance of nature is by reproducing. The number of people in the world is growing at an explosive rate, even as the numbers of many other species dramatically decline. Although it was not until 1800 or so that the earth's population reached one billion, in just two centuries we have brought that total up to five billion. By the year 2100, some people predict, the population will more than double again. Our resources—food, water, shelter, and gainful employment—are already taxed and will not be able to keep pace with this phenomenal growth.

When food and other raw materials for each person begin to disappear more rapidly than they can be replaced, either because of direct environmental damage or from the stress of an exploding human population, people begin to compete fiercely for those that remain. The struggle between groups of people for scarce necessities can easily lead to war.

Nations attempt to work out peaceful agreements among

themselves for the sharing, selling, buying, and swapping of natural resources. Often these agreements occur between rich and poor nations. The wealthier, developed countries typically have depleted their own natural resources in the process of development; thus they bargain with developing countries in order to secure the raw materials they continue to need.

In order to pay for food, industry, educational and social programs, and better roads and transportation, poor countries often gladly sell their most precious treasures. Even so, they must also go into debt. The poorest countries of all need to borrow money just to feed their people. For many of them, interest payments on these debts amount to more than half their total exports each year. And a number of these countries are paying for a civil war at the same time they try to repay their loans and borrow more money to buy weapons and supplies.

Arms sales are a devastating factor. In 1990, $880 billion was spent on weapons and preparations for war, fifteen times the total of all official development assistance. Military purchases by the poorest nations have quintupled in the last thirty years and are now almost triple the humanitarian aid received. Amazingly, less than 10 percent of all foreign aid is for education, health, clean water, shelter, sanitation, family planning, and nutrition. The world's conflicts, directly or indirectly, have an adverse effect on almost every aspect of people's lives.

The industrialized nations convert the raw materials they buy from poorer countries into finished, high-technology man- ufactured products, which are sold to their own citizens and also back to the developing nations. Like anybody else, the people of developing countries are eager to upgrade their lifestyles when they can. They become trapped in a vicious cycle of debt, exporting their primary assets—natural resources—to pay off their debts and to import food, consumer products, and weapons.

When the export in question is made from a threatened or endangered species of animal or plant, environmentalists in the industrialized nations cry out in protest. Yet the truth is that for the poorest of people, struggling just to survive, the idea of having an environmental conscience is too remote from daily life to be seriously considered. To make a fundamental change in how our global resources are protected, a fundamental change must be made in the way responsibilities are shared.

Operating under a sense of desperation and urgency, citizens of developing countries will continue to exploit the environment until they find another way to satisfy their needs. For example, higher oil prices have meant that people in many countries can no longer afford petroleum products for fuel. They have turned back to wood for cooking and heating their homes. Before 1973, when the price of oil was about two dollars a barrel, people who did not live in heavily forested areas would use kerosene and other fuels for cooking and heating their homes. Since then, with oil prices ranging from fifteen to thirty dollars a barrel, they have been forced to use increasingly scarce wood supplies.

While climbing in the Himalaya Mountains in 1985, we tourists were required by law to purchase expensive kerosene to cook our meals. Our Sherpa guides told us that since the people could no longer buy expensive fuel, they have cut almost all their remaining trees. We spent two nights at an emergency aid center in a village almost three miles above sea level. The doctor

I went to visit Curitiba, Brazil, because it had the reputation for solving urban environmental problems with imagination rather than money. In a very poor hilly neighborhood whose dirt streets were too narrow and steep for sanitation trucks, I watched as people brought bags of garbage down to pickup points, where they were given fresh vegetables in exchange. Jaime Lerner, the mayor of this subtropical city, told me that he got the idea for this program while watching a news report. "I had been trying to figure out a way to clean up those hard-to-reach places," he said. "When I saw a report saying that farmers were dumping surplus cabbage, it occurred to me that the city could buy these vegetables and exchange them for garbage, lowering disease and improving diets at the same time."

Lerner's style of government during three terms as mayor has been to come up with simple solutions to problems and involve the local people in bringing those ideas to life. Using this approach, Curitiba has built beautiful parks, inexpensive and fast mass transit, and lots of well-kept housing even as its population has doubled. When Lerner left office in January, he was the most popular mayor in Brazilian history.

EUGENE LINDEN
Time *magazine senior writer*

and nurse were forbidden to build any kind of warming fire, even in the subfreezing weather. All of us had to wear several layers of heavy down-filled clothing, day and night.

In a more tropical area of Ethiopia, Rosalynn and I visited a rare forest of planted eucalyptus trees a few miles from Addis Ababa, the capital city. Regular army troops are stationed there

August 3, 1978

To Prime Minister Begin

This is a private and personal letter, and I would appreciate your honoring its confidentiality. I want to express myself frankly and directly to you personally.

During the past year under your leadership of Israel we have made remarkable progress toward peace. The boldness and leadership qualities exhibited by you and President Sadat have contributed to a new and better relationship between Israel and Egypt which was not anticipated by the rest of the world. In my opinion you are the leader who, in the foreseeable future, can and must continue this progress. You have a strong hold on the government, loyalty among your associates, and the

Declassified excerpt from President Carter's private invitation to Prime Minister Menachem Begin regarding the Camp David peace talks.

Jimmy Carter with Alamin Mohamed Saiyed (left), of the Eritrean People's Liberation Front (EPLF), and Ashegre Yigletu, secretary of the Worker's Party of Ethiopia (PDRE), at the Carter Center.

AP/Wide World Photos

Tired but triumphant, President Carter meets Prime Minister Begin in Tel Aviv after a quick trip to Cairo while he juggles the final settlement points of the peace treaty between Egypt and Israel.

Micha Bar'Am/Magnum Photos, Inc.

Jimmy Carter and Mrs. Dominique de Menil present the Carter-Menil Human Rights Prize to La Vicaría de la Solidaridad, a legal assistance group for political prisoners in Chile. Rick Diamond

Examining the voter registration list at a polling site during the 1989 Panamanian elections. The Carter Center

Checking the election ballots at the Argentina School polling site in Port-au-Prince, Haiti, 1990.
AP/Wide World Photos

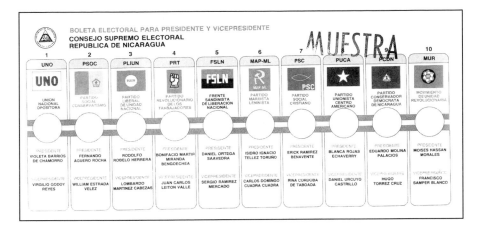

BOLETA ELECTORAL PARA PRESIDENTE Y VICEPRESIDENTE
CONSEJO SUPREMO ELECTORAL
REPUBLICA DE NICARAGUA

MUESTRA

The ballot for president and vice president used in the 1990
Nicaraguan elections.

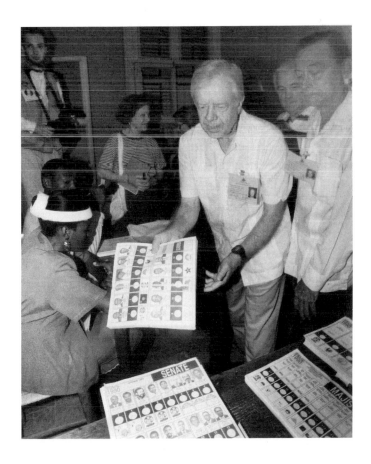

President Carter, newly elected, greets a young supporter at the White House.

Alex Webb/Magnum Photos, Inc.

Hard at work on a Habitat for Humanity site in Washington, D.C.

Dennis Brack/Black Star

Rosalynn Carter hands a baby back to its mother while visiting a Khmer refugee camp at Khao-I-Dang, near the Cambodian border.
AP/Wide World Photos

Rosalynn Carter visits a classroom at Rich's Academy, in Atlanta, part of the Cities-in-Schools project for dropouts and other students having problems in school. AP/Wide World Photos

Jimmy Carter at the 1992 Democratic Convention in Madison Square Garden, New York. Martin Simon/SABA

to insure that no trees are cut. Many people are seen walking from the woods to the city with big bundles of dry limbs and twigs on their backs. This fuel is quite expensive on the streets of the city. In many similar areas without soldiers to guard them, trees are cut down and used until they are gone; women and children then must range farther and farther from their homes to find more trees and sticks to burn. Some of them have told me that they spend six to seven hours a day, traveling many miles, just to obtain wood for cooking fires.

When the land is bared of trees, the unprotected soil erodes rapidly. Water that had previously soaked into the ground runs off into nearby streams, making it impossible for crops to flourish or animals to graze. Famine soon threatens, and rural families are forced to move to the cities. When they leave, their idle farms mean that even less food will be produced, requiring the country to incur more foreign debt in order to feed the people.

It is important to remember that historically the industrialized nations have caused the most damage to the environment, with their careless technology and policies. Emissions from factories, machinery, and vehicles have caused ozone depletion and acid rain. Leaders of the wealthier nations must be willing to accept responsibility for past mistakes and to help shoulder the financial burden for environmental protection that the developing nations cannot afford to carry alone.

In 1992, the United Nations Conference on Environment and Development (UNCED), known as the Earth Summit, was held in Rio de Janeiro, Brazil. It was the first opportunity since a similar conference in Stockholm, Sweden, in 1972, for far-reaching agreements to be made on the world's most serious environmental problems. Unfortunately, barriers between rich and poor countries were not broken down at this meeting. The delegation from the United States was not willing to accept some of the strongest proposals of the summit concerning global warming and ozone depletion. U.S. representatives were also reluctant for wealthier nations to help finance a worldwide effort among all countries for tighter restraints on air pollution and forest harvesting.

The arguments will continue among environmentalists, government agencies, industrialists, farmers, miners, timber companies, and citizens who believe that outdoor areas should be preserved for recreational use. The most damaging conflict of interests may be between the rich industrialized countries and those that are poor and struggling just for existence. Until a more cooperative approach can be evolved among all nations, it is unlikely that much progress will be made in improving the world's environment.

The worst environmental degradation occurs in wars. Fields are abandoned, livestock is destroyed, and governments do not even try to control toxic wastes or the pollution of water, land, or air. Displaced people no longer feel responsible for the quality of life in their own communities. In the recent Gulf War, large quantities of oil were deliberately dumped into the Persian Gulf, and hundreds of oil wells were set on fire and burned for months before they could be extinguished. For hundreds of miles, the sky was covered with thick black smoke. Even in peacetime, armed forces contribute to pollution to a surprising degree. In 1983, for instance, a study revealed that 58 percent of all pollutants from air traffic over West Germany came from military planes.

There are many things we can do to help protect our environment. The Carter Center has begun a program to help conflicting groups understand one another's environmental concerns. Our goal is to work with scientists, timber companies, professional foresters, environmentalists, and government officials to encourage the preservation of irreplaceable rain forests and other woodlands and to replant other harvested trees. Many of the denuded areas of the world can be planted in new species of trees that are fast-growing and put nutrients into the soil, trees whose leaves make food for humans and animals and whose limbs can be removed for firewood while the trees are still growing to maturity. In all these projects, we must help wealthy and poorer nations reach a better understanding of each other's needs so that more effective financial and humanitarian programs can be designed.

The skills learned in resolving political conflicts can be used to help resolve environmental conflicts as well. Working toward consensus, we always stress that peace, human rights, and the environment are interrelated. Poverty-stricken people are understandably more concerned with ending starvation, finding adequate shelter and employment, and ensuring the survival of their children than they are in dealing with environmental issues. But in reality, there is no separation among these concerns. Wherever the environment is ruined beyond repair, human suffering is inevitable. Ecology knows no national boundaries —wealthy nations as well as poor feel the effects of air pollution, soil erosion, silting of streams, global warming, acid rain, ozone depletion, and the loss of biodiversity. A working partnership must be formed so that we can solve these truly universal problems before it is too late.

7

HUMAN RIGHTS

What Rights Do We Share?

In my farewell address as president, I said, "America did not invent human rights. In a very real sense, it was the other way around. Human rights invented America. We were the first nation in the world to be founded on such an idea." This does not mean that the American Revolution immediately brought equal freedom or equal rights to all Americans. Slavery remained lawful. Blacks, Native Americans, women, young people, and those without property were all denied various rights under the law. Yet the driving force behind our identity as a society was a hunger for liberty—a hunger that is leading us step-by-step toward equality of opportunity for all citizens. Many other countries around the world are struggling to make the same kind of progress, and they deserve our support.

It is surprising to most Americans that people in other nations often define human rights almost exclusively as those that sustain life—the right to adequate food, medical care, a home, education, and a job. In the past two chapters, we have discussed several of these rights and how important they are. Yet individual freedoms are the most precious possessions of all in a democracy. Americans are justifiably proud of our Bill of Rights, which guarantees a free press and prevents the government from interfering with our freedoms of expression, assembly, and worship. We cherish our rights to travel freely, to vote, to obtain a fair trial, and even to emigrate from America if we so choose. There is also protection against discrimination based on sex, age, race, or ethnic origin. These are what we define as human rights.

As president, sometimes I had to argue with leaders of Communist countries about which human rights were most important. When I accused them of jailing people without trial, controlling the news media, restricting people's movements, or outlawing religion, they would respond that all their people had homes, medical care, and guaranteed jobs, and that in their countries women had the same rights and duties as men. They would refer to the homeless people on the sidewalks of American cities, our many unemployed citizens, and the high cost of individual medical care. They would charge that we treat minorities like second-class citizens. It was impossible for me to ignore or reject these arguments.

The fact is that everyone deserves all of these human rights. Everyone has a right to a peaceful existence, the basic personal freedoms, the alleviation of suffering, and the opportunity to lead a productive life. I realized that my own voice from the

White House as a world leader would be strengthened if my administration would define human rights in this broad sense, and if we would also admit to the need for improvement in some elements of American life.

I decided that my domestic policy initiatives would focus on the rights of the neediest members of American society, including women, minorities, children, and those families living in poverty or in an unclean or unsafe environment. We created a new Department of Education and insured that every qualified American high school graduate could obtain a college education, regardless of family income. A "superfund," financed by mandatory contributions from chemical companies, was established to clean up toxic waste sites that endangered communities' health. We initiated special assistance for women and infant children to help insure that better nutrition was available before and after childbirth. A strong program was established to immunize our nation's children against diseases. More women and representatives of racial minority groups were appointed to serve as federal judges than in all the previous history of our country. Special laws were passed to protect the rights of handicapped persons, and a presidential directive required equal opportunity for all people, regardless of race, to obtain housing.

Further work needs to be done in almost all these areas of American life. Unfortunately, the plight of families in our inner cities has grown much worse, with increases in juvenile crime, teen pregnancy, school dropout rates, homelessness, and unemployment. Elements of racism and discrimination still exist. Human rights are still being violated in our country. My hope is that individuals, private organizations, religious groups, and government agencies at all levels will work as partners with one another and with low-income families to improve life for our most deprived neighbors.

Americans, in my opinion, should have the right to travel freely without government interference, so I decided to remove all travel restrictions on our citizens and permit them to visit any place in the world that was relatively safe. This order applied even to such countries as Cuba, North Korea, Iraq, Vietnam, and Cambodia, although we had strong arguments and poor relations with these governments. After I left office, the travel restraints were put back into effect.

All American ambassadors who served under me were urged to speak out strongly against human rights abuses in the countries where they were assigned. Persecuted people often came to our embassies for protection. Sometimes these policies caused serious arguments between the oppressors and our government. Foreign leaders knew that when they met with me, we would discuss human rights in their nation and in America. For example, when I met with President Leonid Brezhnev of the Soviet Union to negotiate an agreement on nuclear arms reductions, I spoke to him about political prisoners, the Soviets' refusal to let Jews and others move out of the country, and the restrictions the Soviet government had imposed on people in neighboring eastern Europe. For people in those nations, the ultimate authority for every aspect of life was in Moscow, and not in their own governments. Soviet tanks and soldiers controlled the streets. Each nation's leaders had to be selected or approved by Soviet rulers. Citizens did not enjoy the basic freedoms of speech, assembly, and worship, or the right to move from one job or home to another, or to emigrate to another country. After our talks, many abuses continued, but some progress was forthcoming in the Soviet Union and other countries.

Brezhnev was always quite uncomfortable when I turned our discussion to human rights. If I talked about the release of Jewish dissidents, he attempted to avoid any verbal exchange and would ask his Russian interpreter to hand me a carefully drafted paper that spelled out the official Soviet policy on human rights. One of the most famous Jewish leaders was Anatoly Shcharansky, whose name was always on my list to be discussed. I remember that once, Soviet Foreign Minister Andrei Gromyko said that a Jewish dissident like Shcharansky was just a "microscopic dot who is of no consequence to anyone." Despite their denial of interest in the subject, the Soviet leaders were affected by private and public criticism. There was a dramatic increase in the emigration of Jews from the Soviet Union, from fourteen thousand in 1976 to more than fifty-one thousand in 1979. In addition, public debate of these issues made people around the world more familiar with the subject of human rights.

Partially because of modern radio and television communications, people in many nations have come to understand what freedom and democracy mean and to demand better lives for themselves. Great changes are taking place in Latin America, in the former Soviet Union, in eastern Europe, and in some countries in Africa and Asia. Human rights and new political freedoms usually go hand in hand. There are some exceptions, as we have noted before. Sometimes, when freed from strong military domination, people in a liberated region will turn against one another because of ancient religious and ethnic differences and struggles for land. This is what has occurred in what was Yugoslavia, as Christian Serbs have launched destructive military attacks in order to punish or kill Muslims in Bosnia and Herzegovina. Similar violence has broken out in several of the new nations that formerly were part of the Soviet Union.

There are many laws, constitutional guarantees, and international treaties that are designed to protect the rights of citizens from oppressive leaders. In democracies, human rights abuses can be corrected by voting out of office the leaders who fail to govern properly or by arousing the public with peaceful demonstrations, as America's civil rights and women's rights movements showed.

In too many nondemocratic countries, a ruler who cannot be voted out of office personally determines the rights of citizens. Unstable rulers, fearful of the status of their regimes, or military dictators, unpopular but still powerful, tend to increase repression in order to avoid public criticism and prevent political opponents from recruiting support. In practice, these corrupt leaders, who themselves subvert the law, often control the very people who are responsible for enforcing justice: the police, the armed forces, and the judges.

The Carter Center still attempts to improve health care and assist with the alleviation of starvation among a country's citizens even when a government's human rights standards do not meet our own. If we take away our programs, it is the people who suffer, not the leaders criticized by the international community.

As a recent example, in June of 1989, thousands of Chinese students peacefully gathered in a pro-democracy rally at Tienenman Square in Beijing. When government troops used force to remove them after a week of demonstrations, many young people were killed and several thousand more were arrested.

At the time, the Carter Center was completing two extensive projects in China. One was to train several hundred teachers and counselors in the education of physically and mentally handicapped children. The other was to construct a large factory for the production of artificial arms and legs. We initially withdrew our people, but after the violence ended, we sent them back to continue their work. When the projects were completed, there were more than nine hundred new special-education specialists in China, giving new opportunities to many blind, deaf, and mentally retarded children. Some specialists were in the classrooms themselves, and others were training additional teachers. Thousands of crippled people, many of whom had been confined to their homes, or to the streets as beggars, were being fitted with artificial legs and leading more normal lives.

On my next visit to China, to dedicate the factory and meet the trained counselors, I used the occasion to urge government leaders to grant amnesty to all nonviolent dissidents and to hold no further trials of the Tienenman Square demonstrators. Chinese leaders informed me that there would not be additional trials of the demonstrators and authorized me to announce to the sixty thousand Chinese students in American universities that they would not be arrested or abused if they returned home to live or to visit their families. Since then, the Carter Center has followed up with efforts to protect the rights of individual Chinese citizens, but abuses are likely to continue until the basic policies of the Chinese government are changed.

Another case of extreme human rights abuses is in Sudan. Almost all nations have stopped financial assistance to the country because of the terrible civil war, but in spite of this, the Carter Center has continued its Global 2000 grain production program there. Sudanese farmers increased their wheat production from one hundred thousand tons in 1987 to one million tons in 1992, despite the fighting.

The United States government can restrict its dealings with a country like Sudan when there are human rights violations, but the relationship between human rights and diplomacy is much more complex when a nation like China is involved, with its one billion people and central role in Asia. Trade and political stability in the region are important, and to sever trade and diplomatic relations with China would endanger peace and might very well result in more suffering by the very citizens we wish to protect. The situation is further complicated by the tens of thousands of Chinese students in the United States, most of them doing graduate work in our universities. Although government leaders in Beijing assured me that none of the students would be arrested or charged with crimes, I personally know of at least two cases in which students were arrested upon their return. With our help, they were released, but many other students are still uncertain about what will happen to them if they return home.

The United States of America *must* be the world's champion of human rights. Our history and character as a nation uniquely qualify us for this role, and our enormous influence makes it possible for us to lead effectively. Since the president is, in effect, the voice of our country, oppressed peoples around the world most fear silence from our White House. That same type of silence is what oppressors want most. The world's silence permitted Adolf Hitler to execute millions of innocent people in the Nazi holocaust. Our black neighbors continued to suffer segregation for a hundred years after slavery was abolished

Recipients of the
Carter-Menil Human Rights Prize

1986 YURI ORLOV, Soviet Union, *a Soviet physicist and dissident*
GRUPO DE APOYO MUTUO, Guatemala, *a human rights group founded by relatives of the disappeared*

1987 LA VICARÍA DE LA SOLIDARIDAD, Chile, *a group that provides legal assistance to political prisoners and also helps the families of victims of human rights abuses*

1988 THE SISULU FAMILY, South Africa, *leading activists in the fight against apartheid*

1989 AL-HAQ, West Bank, *a Palestinian human rights organization*
B'TSELEM/THE ISRAELI INFORMATION CENTER FOR HUMAN RIGHTS IN THE OCCUPIED TERRITORIES, Israel, *an Israeli human rights group monitoring the treatment of Palestinians in the occupied territories*

1990 THE CONSEJO DE COMUNIDADES ETNICAS RUNUJEL JUNAM, Guatemala, *a group of Mayan Indians who monitor and defend human rights and fundamental freedoms*

because many southerners, including myself as a young person, failed to speak out strongly against racial discrimination.

Even today, there are countless examples in our own country and around the world of direct abuse and of indirect discrimination that call out for correction. Many organizations have been formed to detect and expose these cases. Among them are Amnesty International, committees of doctors and lawyers, and specialists who observe or "watch" different regions of the world, such as Helsinki Watch, Americas Watch, Asia Watch, Africa

THE CIVIL RIGHTS MOVEMENT OF SRI LANKA, *a nonpartisan, interethnic organization committed to the promotion and protection of civil and political rights*

1991   FATHER IGNACIO ELLACURÍA, S.J., El Salvador

FATHER IGNACIO MARTÍN BARÓ, S.J., El Salvador

FATHER SEGUNDO MONTES MOZO, S.J., El Salvador

FATHER JUAN RAMÓN MORENO PARDO, S.J., El Salvador

FATHER AMANDO LÓPEZ QUINTANA, S.J., El Salvador

FATHER JOAQUÍN LÓPEZ Y LÓPEZ, S.J., El Salvador

These Jesuit priests were slain on November 16, 1989. The award was made in their honor to the University of Central America.

1992   HAITIAN REFUGEE CENTER, United States, *founded to protect the civil and constitutional rights of Haitians seeking refuge in the U.S.*

NATIVE AMERICAN RIGHTS FUND, United States, *a national advocacy group specializing in Indian law that provides legal representation for Native Americans*

Watch, and Middle East Watch. Our human rights group at the Carter Center works with all these organizations and assists with some of the most serious cases.

In addition to working with many human rights organizations and interceding directly to prevent human rights abuses, we attempt to publicize these crimes and to honor human rights heroes. Each year we give one or two awards to people, or organizations, who are most courageous and effective in this difficult work. Known as the Carter-Menil Human Rights Prize,

On quiet days, when nothing is happening, the job involves driving all over the assigned region, visiting the camps and villages, talking to people, and trying to get a general idea about the Israeli presence in the area. We work until dark. We all have radios that keep us in contact with the Jerusalem office, and if there is a report or rumor that something is happening somewhere—a patrol has just arrested someone; there has been a shooting; stones are being thrown—we are sent to investigate. Quite often there is a curfew, but we are allowed in anyway and can survey the scene to determine what is happening; why; and what, if anything, can be done to minimize human rights abuses.

The thing that has my brain churning the most these days is how complicated the whole situation is. There is Israeli-Arab tension, Christian-Jewish-Muslim tension, Sunni-Shiite tension, Druze-Arab tension, fundamentalist-progressive tension, PLO-PFLP-Hamas tension . . . and of course, immediately upon arrival in the midst of all of this, one is pressed very hard to take sides.

JAMES T. LESTER III
a United Nations Relief and Works Agency (UNRWA)
refugee affairs officer in the West Bank

they are accompanied by a gift of $100,000 to assist the recipients in their work.

In the future, the Carter Center program will expend more effort on helping emerging democracies to write proper laws protecting their citizens, strengthening private human rights groups within these countries, exposing regimes earlier when they begin to violate international standards, and finding better ways for abused people to let their plight be known.

Some member countries of the UN have been quite critical of United States laws that allow the death penalty (especially for juveniles) and our use of military force to accomplish our goals in other countries or regions. Our bombing and shelling of villages around Beirut, Lebanon, in 1982; our invasions of Grenada and Panama; and our sponsoring the Contra War in Nicaragua are mentioned frequently in debates with other nations about their own human rights policies or warlike actions. The United States demands that other countries refrain from developing nuclear explosives but has insisted on its right to continue development and testing. Other nuclear powers, like Russia and France, have decided to stop testing altogether.

In 1992, the U.S. Congress mandated that nuclear testing be stopped until July 1993, but President George Bush announced that such tests could then be resumed until 1996. It is clear that there must be a common agreement among the major nuclear powers in order for all testing of nuclear explosives to be banned, and that leadership from Washington will be required. The issue is still in doubt.

As the world community has begun to move together to take advantage of opportunities in the post–cold war era, the number of conflicts and challenges on the United Nations' agenda has grown. This is a healthy expansion of the role of international organizations. Sometimes, people who seek to find peace and an end to the suffering in their own troubled countries can do so only with outside assistance.

8

MEDIATION

Negotiating a Win-Win Settlement

World War I was the deadliest war ever when it occurred. By the time an armistice was declared, in 1918, more than eight million lives had been lost on the battlefields of Europe. When the victorious Allies met in Paris shortly thereafter to negotiate and draft peace agreements, they levied heavy penalties on the defeated Germany, Austria-Hungary, and Turkey, splitting these empires into smaller, less-powerful nations.

The Paris Peace Conference of 1919 may have been the first time in history when a group of world leaders acknowledged to one another that warfare had grown too devastating to be a practical way of resolving international disputes. Hoping to prevent future wars, these leaders planned to form a League of Nations. The member countries of the league would agree to limit armaments, to help defend one another against aggression, and to provide a forum where international conflicts could be argued and resolved peacefully. However, this idea was severely weakened when the U.S. Senate, arguing that America would be tied too closely to European events beyond our control, rejected President Woodrow Wilson's urgent request to join the league. Despite the league's noble ambitions, war broke out in Europe again just twenty years later, soon drawing in other nations from around the world—including the United States. World War II is estimated to have cost more than thirty-five million lives.

Why did the treaties reached after World War I fail to establish a permanent peace? Some historians argue that the agreements of the Paris Peace Conference actually created the instability that led to World War II. Because of the harsh terms of the Treaty of Versailles, Germany went into a deep economic depression that lasted through the 1920s and 1930s. Popular despair, resentment, and ambition helped Adolf Hitler come to power. Hitler's government became ever more dictatorial and oppressive, and his aggressive politics eventually culminated in the invasion of Poland in 1939. Italy and Japan joined Germany in its aggression, and the three countries became aligned as the Axis powers of World World II. The tough we win–you lose settlement drafted at the Paris Peace Conference had failed to preserve the peace. When the Allies finally won another victory in this second world war and began to consider their options for peace, they tried to avoid repeating this mistake.

The post–World War II negotiators again divided Germany. They also abolished the totalitarian governments of Germany, Italy, and Japan and placed military restraints on the defeated nations to prevent them from attacking their weaker neighbors. Although these steps were punitive, at the same time the people of the three countries were given an opportunity to prosper under democratic governments of their own. The United States also provided massive financial aid to help Europe overcome the ravages of war. As the new democracies prospered, they joined with the Allies and others in the United Nations, and peace among the world's major nations has been maintained during the last fifty years.

As discussed earlier in the book, the vast majority of the world's many conflicts since then have been civil wars. These conflicts are typically started by rebels who may have any of a variety of goals: to end persecution, to secede or to be self-governing within the nation's boundaries, to have more political authority in the government that exists, or to have greater economic power.

Political leaders of opposing nations who wish to resolve an *international* dispute may turn to the United Nations for assistance. Other formal groups of nations—especially the Organization of American States (OAS), the Organization of African Unity (OAU), the Commonwealth of Nations, and the Arab League—are also playing an increasing role in promoting international peace in their regions. For warring factions that wish to end a *civil* dispute, however, the forum for debate is not always as obvious. Except in special circumstances, international organizations are prevented by law and custom from meeting or communicating directly with revolutionaries trying to change or overthrow the government of a member nation.

In 1987, I met at the Carter Center with the secretaries-general of the United Nations, the Organization of American States,

International Negotiation Network Council

JIMMY CARTER, *council chair, former president of the United States*

OSCAR ARIAS SÁNCHEZ, *former president of Costa Rica*

OLUSEGUN OBASANJO, *former head of state of Nigeria*

LISBET PALME, *chair, Swedish Committee for UNICEF*

JAVIER PERÉZ DE CUÉLLAR, *former secretary-general of the United Nations*

SHRIDATH RAMPHAL, *chair, West Indian Commission*

MARIE-ANGÉLIQUE SAVANÉ, *former special adviser, United Nations High Commissioner for Refugees*

EDUARD SHEVARDNADZE, *former foreign minister of the Soviet Union; president, Republic of Georgia*

DESMOND TUTU, *Anglican archbishop of Cape Town, South Africa*

CYRUS VANCE, *former United States secretary of state*

ELIE WIESEL, *director, Elie Wiesel Foundation for Humanity*

ANDREW YOUNG, *former United States ambassador to the United Nations*

and the Commonwealth of Nations to discuss the problems of dispute resolution. Although we realized that almost all the conflicts in the world today are within nations, the participants made it plain that their charters would continue to limit their assistance only to international conflicts. It was after this meeting that the Carter Center launched the International Negotiation Network (INN), to seek peaceful ways to reduce civil conflicts and to prevent smaller-scale disputes from escalating into wars.

MEDIATION AND WIN-WIN SETTLEMENTS

The INN attempts to link different peacemaking resources across the globe. Our organization also helps bring attention to conflicts that are not being addressed by world leaders and that may have been relatively ignored by the news media. Just as importantly, the INN helps spread the message that war is no longer an acceptable way of resolving a dispute.

Because of hatred and mistrust, disputing parties often find it very difficult to communicate constructive ideas or proposals. They may not even agree to meet each other face-to-face. A trusted third party can sometimes help by carrying ideas back and forth and by putting forward new proposals, step-by-step, until both sides accept them. This process of third-party negotiation is called mediation.

Agreement on every item, no matter how small or insignificant, must be voluntary and unanimous if an effective settlement is to be reached. If one side forces undesirable concessions on the other, then the cease-fire or peace is not likely to last. If both contenders, however, feel that they have gained more than they have lost from the process, the outcome is a *win-win* settlement—and peace may prove to be permanent.

Camp David is a good example of how two parties worked to resolve a long-standing conflict with the help of a third party, although it was also an exceptional situation. Negotiations to resolve conflicts rarely occur directly between leaders; usually teams of political advisers and experts do the talking, reporting their progress back to top officials. At Camp David, we were three heads of state, and we secluded ourselves for nearly two weeks to hammer out a peace agreement. Even though political, cultural, historical, and religious differences had to be overcome, we were able to explore areas of possible agreement and keep the talks going until a framework for peace was reached.

At the Carter Center, we have improved upon the mediating procedures used at Camp David. The INN has learned many lessons the hard way—by trial and error. Our biggest successes have come when we have encouraged other countries to follow the principles of democracy, like holding free and fair elections. We'll hear more about that in the next chapter. As approaches to conflict resolution have changed worldwide, mediation services like ours are becoming better known and more in demand. The INN receives many requests for help from around the world, but most of them are from just one side in a dispute— usually from the side that believes it is going to lose. To participate successfully, our role must be supported by all the major parties involved in the conflict. Sometimes we ourselves seek the necessary invitations.

Potential mediators have to be well acquainted with the biases and opinions of each party involved. They must be patient, understanding, and neutral enough to be trusted by both sides. In addition to the mediators, observers who are known and trusted by both disputants sometimes watch the proceedings. These observers can be helpful in gaining and maintaining the disputants' faith in the integrity of the talks.

Almost always, the first steps in a peace effort are the most difficult. Some of the important work is done before any formal discussions can begin. We call this premediation, or talks-about-talks. Even when both sides are ready to seek peace, they must agree on who should convene the talks, where and when the process should begin, and what issues will be discussed. There are always questions about who should represent the opposing forces, who should mediate, whether the discussions will be secret or publicized, what observers may attend, what records will be kept, and when and by whom reports are to be released to the public.

Particularly when the conflict involves a rebel ethnic group with its own culture and dialect, the choice of languages can be a crucial political issue. A third, neutral language may sometimes be used to avoid one side's having to agree to speak the other's language. When we were negotiating with the Iranians to release American hostages in January 1981, we had to use three languages: English, Farsi (the language of Iran), and French (the language of the Algerian intermediaries). At the Camp David summit with Egypt and Israel, we discussed issues in English, which was the official language, but the final documents were also written in Arabic and Hebrew.

Some revolutionary groups composed of farmers and other working people with no experience in diplomacy have no concept of the meaning of words used in peace talks. In a negotiation I assisted, one negotiating team insisted that to *mediate* was to *dominate;* that *compromise* meant *total surrender;* and that an *observer* was an active *negotiator*. We could make progress only by including the dictionary definitions in the written texts.

One important early task in any negotiation is to create a framework for the discussion. This clear outline of the topics to be covered will give all parties the sense that they may achieve their separate goals without beginning or continuing a war. If preparations are successful, the potential negotiators will feel that they can participate without being embarrassed or losing face.

There are many mediation techniques available. One that we like at the Carter Center is to use a single text. After premediation work is completed, the third party puts a clear and direct proposal down on paper, incorporating the most important interests of both sides with some options for compromise. Then, from this draft document, the mediator gathers suggestions and criticisms from each side. A revised draft is prepared, and the document is reviewed again. This process, which I first used at Camp David, is repeated as long as necessary, ideally until full agreement is reached.

Even if both sides cannot accept the final document and ultimately no agreement is reached, the points they accept and the remaining differences become much clearer to everyone concerned during this process. A powerful, sometimes unanticipated factor that can force compromises is the realization that each side's negative positions are likely to be disclosed to the public and, most importantly, to their own supporters. This puts pressure on the negotiators, because they know they are likely to be condemned if they let the war continue for unsound or minor reasons.

The search for peace is worth the effort, no matter how formidable the obstacles might be. One of the most formidable obstacles of all can be the continuing conviction of one or both sides that they might still win the war. This was a problem we faced when the Carter Center conducted mediations between Ethiopia and Eritrea.

Ethiopia, a nation of northeast Africa that dates back over two thousand years, is both one of the oldest and poorest countries in the world. Its society has always been divided into small regional groups. One of these regions is Eritrea, in the north along the Red Sea coast. Another is Tigray, located inland from Eritrea. Both the Eritreans and the Tigrayans had armies that had been fighting against the central government forces for many years.

More than a million people had perished in these civil wars, either from weapons in battle or from exposure or starvation caused by the conflict. In 1988, I went to the region and convinced Ethiopian President Mengistu Haile Mariam and the leaders of the Eritrean and Tigrayan groups opposing him to begin peace talks, hoping that a cease-fire would lead to permanent treaties and an end to the devastation and suffering. It was later decided that Italian officials in Rome would conduct the talks with the Tigrayans, while the Eritrean leaders and President Mengistu's representatives would come to Atlanta.

When the two groups first convened in Atlanta, the Carter Center had already conducted a year's research on the conflict, including fact-finding missions in the country itself. One of the main things we had learned was that total success would be almost impossible. Neither side was prepared to believe they would lose militarily. Old issues were still burning strongly and would be very difficult to resolve. Most Eritreans wanted total independence from Ethiopia, to be granted through an internationally monitored referendum on self-determination among their people. Since Eritrea included all the seacoast, this would leave the rest of Ethiopia completely landlocked, without direct access to the ocean. The Tigrayans and their allies—with the exception of the Eritreans—preferred to remain an integral part of Ethiopia, but demanded that Mengistu's Communist regime be replaced with a democratic government with all leaders chosen through free and fair elections. Despite these points of fundamental disagreement, we decided to proceed.

To make the discussions as informal and comfortable as possible, we created a setting at the Carter Center almost like a living room. The representatives of the two parties sat facing each other across small coffee tables, while the Carter Center team sat on one end of the room to form a horseshoe shape. Both parties wanted us to tape-record all comments. Although everyone knew English, the Eritreans insisted on speaking their own language, Arabic, and the Ethiopians, Amharic. The translations took a lot of time, but we knew we were making progress later in the talks when the participants forgot themselves and broke into English.

The purpose of the Atlanta talks was to set the agenda for the main talks to come later. Preliminary issues included how much publicity there would be, how records would be kept, who would preside over the meetings, and who would observe. Even small details had to be settled, such as which participants would approve the exact wording of the final statement at the end of the Atlanta talks.

For twelve days the parties met with us in full sessions or in smaller groups to debate these questions. During the constant discussions, I used my laptop computer to record the points as we discussed them. The words in every sentence were debated, and I would print out a new version every time it seemed we had reached an agreement. There were often several negotiators gathered around my computer screen as I typed, reading over my shoulder and making comments. Despite a lot of tension between the delegations, no one ever walked out. When we

One evening, during the negotiations between the Ethiopians and the Eritreans at the Carter Center, we were sitting on the patio having dinner. It was a beautiful night. The stars were bright, the city lights glowing in the distance. Members of each delegation sat at my small table. The "enemies" were laughing and talking about their families and about being in the United States when we heard an airplane flying overhead. Suddenly, one of the Eritrean men was under the table. He immediately got up and apologized, very embarrassed. He said, "Please excuse me, but in my country when an airplane flies over, it drops bombs." It was shocking, and I realized how far away and how impersonal war in Africa is to me, to us.

We began to talk about his country and how the people had to live underground because of the war. Even schools and hospitals were underground. He also told me that everyone had to fight, men and women. If a woman got pregnant, she would fight until it was time for the baby to come. She would have three months at home to be with her child before she had to go back to the battlefield. Then someone too old to fight or who had been crippled in the war would take care of the baby!

This was the Eritrean way of life for thirty years. At long last, they now are on the road to peace.

ROSALYNN CARTER

began to feel discouraged, we reminded ourselves that these negotiators in Atlanta were doing their best to represent communities in which hundreds of thousands of citizens had been killed. The Ethiopians reminded us that peace talks had been under way between them and Somalians for more than ten years, and they had never reached agreement on even an agenda. Comparatively speaking, we made good progress.

We adjourned our Atlanta sessions having settled all but three agenda items: who would chair the main peace talks, who would observe, and who would serve as staff. Both sides agreed to let me choose the time and place for the next round of negotiations, and I decided that Nairobi, Kenya, would be the most convenient site. We reconvened two months later, hoping that we could resolve the three remaining agenda items. We held a few formal meetings with the complete delegations, but the harmony established in Atlanta was gone. When in each other's presence, the two groups would only condemn each other and not seek agreement. We had gotten close to the main controversial issues, and every decision at the negotiating table would have a profound effect on the lives of the people they represented. The delegations were now more tightly controlled by their absent leaders than they had been in Atlanta. Tensions were so high that most of the time I had to meet separately with one leader or group and then the other.

Although Rosalynn and I and our INN group in the end spent more than twenty days and nights in our efforts, we were ultimately unsuccessful in reaching a complete and final agreement. Fighting resumed, and the Tigrayan forces, joined by warriors from other regions, eventually reached the capital city of Addis Ababa in May 1991, forcing the president of Ethiopia to leave the country. During these three years, I met frequently with Meles Zinawe, the Tigrayan military commander, and became quite friendly with him. He was a popular leader, and he pledged to his people that he would bring freedom, democracy, and economic reform to the nation. He also agreed that the Eritreans could have a referendum to decide for themselves the status of their region. It is almost certain that by the time this book is published this decision will have been made, and Eritrea will be a new and independent nation.

I have been back to Ethiopia several times at President Meles's request. The Carter Center is helping the new government with health policies, food production, human rights issues, establishment of a court system, and the planning of democratic elections. With people from the different regions still struggling against one another over ethnic issues and for political advantage, the country's future is still in doubt. But at least peace is being given a chance.

The conflicting goals, mutual distrust, and changing political and military situations in Ethiopia prevented a neat ending to the talks we sponsored. Yet we still helped to achieve a cease-fire in the country for over a year—and let the different groups begin to understand and acknowledge one another, a crucial step for the eventual democratization of the country.

9

ELECTIONS

The Road to Democracy

The founders of our nation devised a complicated system of government that has endured for more than two hundred years. They believed that only if the citizens themselves had control over the reins of government would they be protected from tyrants or dictators who might try to take away their rights. The more broadly governmental power was shared, the more secure the rights of the people would be.

Thus they created three separate branches of government—executive, legislative, and judicial—to share the power of governing. They also adopted a written constitution, a permanent body of law that gave each organ of government its certain unique responsibilities as well as a degree of control over the actions of the others. Added to the Constitution was the Bill of

Rights, which guaranteed certain freedoms directly to the American people.

The continuing success of American democracy depends upon maintaining four vital aspects of the Founding Fathers' design: a free and fair elections system, an independent judiciary, civilian authority over the military, and an independent news media. These institutions protect Americans from tyranny on many levels. Of these, the single most important safeguard of all is the right to vote—the right to endorse our leaders or to change them when they no longer faithfully represent our needs and wishes.

As a famous theologian, Reinhold Niebuhr, said, "Man's capacity for justice makes democracy possible, but man's inclination to injustice makes democracy necessary." Americans can achieve justice and control corrupt or abusive leaders through our democratic elections—by voting them out of office. Yet in countries where there are no free and fair elections, the people have no power to change a despotic or repressive regime. They sometimes cannot even voice their opposition to the government in public without breaking the law.

Free elections are a way to let citizens correct injustices without forcing them to resort to violence. In countries where no elections are held, it is usually true that the president or ruler has sole control over the military and the courts. This means that should a group of citizens attempt to change the government by demonstrating their displeasure or by other means, they must confront the national army or police. If and when the protesters are arrested or captured, they have little guarantee of a fair hearing or trial.

Sometimes opposition parties that are not equipped to launch a revolution resort to acts of terrorism to threaten the incumbents. For strategic reasons of their own, other countries or outside groups may join in the fight, offering support or arms to one of the parties involved. A country's internal political problems can eventually erupt into civil war and even into a full-scale regional conflict. An election system that insures a peaceful transfer of power from leader to leader is an excellent way to prevent or resolve these kinds of conflicts.

Introducing democracy in a country where a strong regime has already taken hold is a difficult task. Few despotic leaders are willing to relinquish their absolute power just for the sake of principle. International pressure or severe internal chaos can help them change their minds, yet often these forces only provoke more oppression. The best time for a move to democracy is when these leaders believe that they are popular enough for a majority of people to vote for them. At the Carter Center, we have developed methods and procedures to help willing governments move toward democracy by holding elections that will be considered free and fair by the contending political parties.

In 1986, fourteen people who, at one time or another, had all been elected leaders of governments in our hemisphere met with me at the Carter Center to discuss democratization and human rights in Latin America and the Caribbean. This group formed the Council of Freely Elected Heads of Government. Since then, sometimes working with other organizations, such as the National Democratic Institute, the United Nations, the Organization of American States, and the Commonwealth of Nations, we have monitored elections in six different countries. The Carter Center also monitors elections in Africa.

What do our observers look for in determining whether an election is free and fair?

- First, if the country is at war, a cease-fire must be called so political campaigns can be conducted. Soldiers should disarm, move into camps, or return to their home polling places. Voters and observers must be able to travel to the polls in safety.
- A large number of local citizens must be trained as election officials and poll watchers, ideally as many as needed to send at least one such person to every voting site. Unbiased observers from other nations also can be extremely useful in ferreting out corruption in the voting process.
- Candidates must be free to qualify for the election in accordance with laws and procedures acceptable to the major political parties. All candidates should have fair access to newspapers and to television and radio advertising. In countries where the incumbent government traditionally controls the media, observers should watch this aspect of the election very carefully.
- A complete and accurate list of the names of citizens who are currently qualified to vote in the election must be compiled.
- There must be a guarantee that the votes are cast freely and then counted accurately. When we observe an election, our poll watchers make a quick report of the results in about 10 percent of the country's polling places. These sites are chosen secretly and carefully to represent the entire vote. We call this a quick count. Then we check these tallies with the nationally

reported results. Our sample results are quite accurate. If there is a significant discrepancy between the numbers, we know that somehow misinformation has reached the national counting headquarters, and the results must be checked closely to determine if the errors are honest ones or if the election must be condemned as fraudulent.

Let's take a look at a few of the elections the Carter Center has monitored and how they have met these requirements. As you read these behind-the-scenes accounts, think carefully about how these election stories may have been portrayed on the nightly news at the time.

PANAMA

Of all Latin American countries, Panama has the closest ties to the United States. We helped the Panamanian people gain their independence from Colombia. We built the canal across their country that joins the Pacific Ocean to the Atlantic Ocean and share the responsibility for its operation. We have worked in harmony on many economic and political issues. In fact, Panamanians have always used U.S. dollars in addition to their own currency. Our two countries did have serious disagreements concerning the control of the Panama Canal, but while I was president, we negotiated new and fairer treaties resolving our problems. Panama at that time was not a democracy—a military dictator, Omar Torrijos, was in power. He pledged to change Panama to a democratic nation.

After I left office, that Panamanian leader was killed in a plane crash. Later, another military commander, General Manuel Noriega, took control. General Noriega attempted to stop all progress toward freedom and democracy, ruling the country in such illegal and corrupt ways that the international community condemned his regime, and his own people put great pressure on him for governmental reform. As is often the case with dictators, he was surrounded by officials who told him exactly what he wanted to hear. At the same time, his critics were afraid to speak publicly for fear of being punished. Convinced that his candidates would win an election without trouble, and wanting the results to be accepted, Noriega asked me to monitor the process. The elections were scheduled for May 7, 1989.

With some reluctance and delay, he accepted our guidelines. The United States government was not involved at this point. No official representative would meet with Noriega or any of his officials. The reasons for this were complicated. Noriega had been closely associated with the U.S. government while he was helping President Reagan in his support of the Contra army that was fighting against the Sandinistas in Nicaragua. When the general shifted his allegiance to the Sandinistas, U.S. officials did everything possible to punish and embarrass him. As a private citizen, I could communicate with him.

Just two days before the election, Rosalynn and I met with Noriega in his closely guarded military headquarters. He was not planning to change his role as the military leader and behind-the-scenes dictator. He would not run for office himself but had put forward a list of handpicked candidates. Convinced of his own great popularity, he was obviously incapable of considering that his personal choices for high office might lose. Despite my insistence, Noriega would not pledge to accept any voting results that might go against him, saying the question was irrelevant.

Despite our concerns about his attitude, we felt confident that we had an accurate enough list of registered voters, and Noriega assured us that our observers would be able to carry out their duties freely.

On election day, the voters were excited to be participating in a truly free and honest election. Many of them stood in line for hours, and by the end of the day, over eight hundred thousand people had voted, about three-quarters of those eligible. It was clear from our observations at the polls and a quick count by the Catholic church that Noriega's candidates were losing by a three-to-one margin. We were sure that the general was also aware of these results. It was reported to me that his men, in civilian clothes but carrying weapons, were going to some of the voting places and seizing the ballots and tally sheets. I visited some of these sites during the night and found the rumors to be true.

Throughout the next morning, I met with the opposition candidates and with other Panamanian leaders. Using the telephone and messengers who went back and forth, I tried to convince Noriega to accept the election results, but without success. At about 2:00 P.M., he stopped answering me. His soldiers, who had previously been quite friendly, barred me from the election headquarters where the ballots and tally sheets from the various regions were supposed to be brought. Later, some organized bands dressed in civilian clothing threw large rocks at my automobile as we drove down the streets.

I was present at a big auditorium ceremony when the national election commission began to announce their first results. According to these reports, the candidates from Noriega's party were winning by a two-to-one margin. The real tally sheets, which we had examined the previous night as votes were tabulated, were filled out very carefully, and each had at least ten different signatures of the polling officials and observers from the different political parties. The ones now being used were only partially complete, with most of them showing just the total vote counts. Furthermore, none of them had more than three signatures, all of which had obviously been written by the same person.

Very angry, I pushed my way onto the stage and shouted in my high school Spanish, "Are you honest officials or thieves? You are stealing the election from the people of Panama!" The general's troops restricted me to my hotel and would not allow me to cross the street to where many international news reporters had gathered. Eventually we got word to the media, and a group of them came over to my hotel. In a press statement, I announced that the government has stolen the election by fraud and that the Panamanian people had been robbed.

Although General Noriega never actually declared his candidates the winners, he officially nullified the election results. This prevented the real winners from taking office. The Organization of American States condemned this violation of human rights, and the United States and some other nations imposed sanctions against Panama. U.S. government leaders seemed determined to drive Noriega out of power. After severe economic pressure on the country failed to make the general step down, U.S. troops stormed Panama in late 1989. Noriega was finally found and arrested, but only after twenty-five American soldiers and at least one thousand Panamanians were killed, and severe economic damage had resulted from the fighting. Top officials who had been honestly elected were installed in office, including Guillermo Endara as president. According to news reports, most Panamanians were happy about the results of the U.S. action, although the United Nations General Assembly called it a "flagrant violation of international law," and the OAS "deeply deplored" the invasion. As with most wars, opinions about the invasion were sharply divided. Had the election process been completed successfully, this conflict and destruction would almost certainly have been avoided.

NICARAGUA

Nicaragua, like Panama, has had a long and sometimes troubled relationship with the United States. For about twenty years in the early part of this century, U.S. armed forces occupied the country and controlled Nicaragua's politics. Before our troops left, in 1933, they had helped Nicaragua establish its own national guard. To serve as commandant of the guard, Nicaraguan president Juan Sacasa appointed Anastasio Somoza Garcia, who was married to his niece.

In 1936, Somoza became dictator of Nicaragua and ruled until he was assassinated, in 1956. His sons then took over, until his youngest, Anastasio Somoza Debayle, was overthrown by a popular uprising in 1979. Until February 1990, Nicaragua had never conducted an election in which all the parties participated and both the winners and the losers respected the results.

The revolutionaries who overthrew the last Somoza called themselves Sandinistas. They flirted with communism as their governing philosophy and formed close ties with Cuba. Many non-Communist Nicaraguans came to oppose the Sandinistas, and a group of counterrevolutionaries called the Contras organized a military operation against them. The United States government supported the Contras, backing them in a war from 1982 to 1989. During this conflict and an accompanying economic embargo, the nation's economy was severely harmed and thirty-five thousand casualties occurred. While the war was going on, the U.S. government rarely communicated with the Sandinistas.

Although the Sandinistas won an election in 1984 that was observed by a few representatives of the OAS, their major opponents withdrew from the campaign shortly before it ended. The United States refused to accept the results of the election. Political forces in their own country, combined with U.S. economic sanctions and support for the Contras, convinced the Sandinistas to schedule another election for 1989, a year earlier than required by the constitution.

In the summer of 1988, I accepted an invitation from Nicaraguan president Daniel Ortega, the opposition parties, and the national election commission for the Council of Freely Elected Heads of Government to serve as observers. Eventually other observers from the United Nations and the Organization of American States joined our council in Nicaragua, hoping to assure a free, fair, and safe election. During the process of determining election rules, we used a number of the mediation techniques discussed in the previous chapter.

Fourteen opposition parties had agreed to a coalition called the National Opposition Union (UNO), and became the Sandinistas' major rival. At least one member of our council visited Nicaragua every week or two to meet with the election commission, the Sandinistas, and UNO. When a crisis arose that these three groups could not resolve, and the two parties would no longer meet with each other, I myself would go back and forth between them (as I have between parties in other peace talks). There were several issues that threatened the successful conduct of the election.

One problem was that the Sandinista government controlled the nation's television and radio media. UNO candidates were having problems presenting their statements and paid advertisements to the public. Although the Sandinistas still had an advantage, we worked out a reasonable compromise. Every week, a certain amount of free time on television and the major radio stations was allotted to each candidate. Of the three major newspapers, two were controlled by the Sandinistas and one by UNO. No attempt was made to grant free advertisements in this news medium. Although not perfect, all the major candidates accepted the arrangement.

Another crisis occurred when people were physically attacked during campaign rallies. One innocent bystander was killed when groups of supporters confronted each other during an UNO rally. We needed to figure out a way to keep political demonstrations from leading to violence. After consulting with party leaders from both sides, we drafted an agreement that spelled out how schedules could be designed so that two rallies would never take place at the same time, what security inspections would be made ahead of time, and how close Sandinista police could come to the crowd. Afterward, observers were usually present to assure that the adopted agreements were honored, and there were no more serious problems at political rallies.

By election day, all the major candidates agreed to accept the outcome of the election, whatever it might be. One more crisis struck, however. On election day, voters were required to dip a finger in indelible ink. Poll officials and observers would be able to notice the mark on anyone who tried to vote twice. About noon, someone discovered that the ink could be washed off easily with Clorox. UNO accused the Sandinistas of trying to cheat, and that afternoon, while voting was still under way, both threatened to withdraw from the election. I quickly met with the leaders and was able to convince them to proceed. Fortunately, at that time both sides still thought they would win, so they agreed to continue. The voting, in the end, was completed successfully.

Results showed that 80 percent of the registered voters went to the polls, and the UNO candidates won by almost a 14 percent margin. The Sandinistas were surprised at their defeat and were reluctant to turn over the reins of government to their adversaries. They had three major concerns, any of which could potentially lead to conflict if not resolved. First, they were concerned about the heavily armed Contras, who would be returning to Nicaragua from their military stations in Honduras now that UNO had won. The Sandinistas wanted to be sure the Sandinista army, soon to be the nation's, would be allowed to protect them from their former enemies. Their second concern was whether the United States would assist the UNO leaders in requiring the Contras to disarm before allowing them to return to Nicaragua. A third issue was how much of the property the Sandinistas and other revolutionaries had seized from the Somozas they would be able to retain. I mediated between UNO and the Sandinistas during the next two days and helped both sides write and sign a carefully worded joint statement.

For the first time in Nicaragua, power was transferred peacefully from the incumbent to a rival after a free and fair election. And for the first time in the world, a revolutionary regime that came to power through armed struggle turned over control of the government to its adversaries as a result of voters' choice. The elections in Nicaragua were truly a historic moment for democracy.

HAITI

In July of 1990, at the request of the acting president of Haiti, Ertha Pascal Trouillot, I went to the capital city of Port-au-Prince to discuss how a peaceful election might be held in that country. Neither the early nor the recent history of the country offered much encouragement to those who hoped for progress toward freedom and peace.

The second-oldest republic in this hemisphere, Haiti had never known real democracy. Beginning in 1957, the country was ruled for thirty years by "Papa Doc" Duvalier and later by his son, "Baby Doc." The militant followers marshaled as a private army of the Duvaliers and known as the Tontons Macoutes terrorized the Haitian people. The popular uprising against this corrupt regime finally forced Baby Doc and his family to leave the country in 1986, and an election was scheduled for the following year. After all the preparations were made, thirty-four of the voters who lined up at one polling place in Port-au-Prince on election day were brutally massacred by the Tontons Macoutes. The Haitian army leaders (who may have been involved in the attack) seized the chance to call off the election, closing the polls just three hours after they opened. Many people were understandably reluctant ever to go to the polls again after that incident.

Working with the National Democratic Institute, our Council of Freely Elected Heads of Government helped the Haitian leaders prepare for another election, planned for December 1990. New and more progressive army leaders seemed to be in support of the electoral process, and the Tontons Macoutes were subdued.

A few months before the election, one of Baby Doc Duvalier's former ministers, Roger Lafontant, who had been accused of inciting the 1987 election violence, came back to Haiti and began to arouse the Macoutes with fiery speeches that threatened the candidates. A special target was a young Catholic priest, Jean-Bertrand Aristide, who was a spokesman for Haiti's poorest people. Lafontant, although charged with many crimes, including murder, was not arrested, because he was always surrounded by a formidable group of a hundred bodyguards and obviously had the support of the Tontons Macoutes.

Despite the risks, eleven candidates qualified to run for president. Lafontant and two other candidates of the Macoutes were disqualified and threatened to disrupt the elections. We were able to help with a successful voter registration process. Because there were so many candidates, it was unlikely that any one person would win a majority of the votes. Yet when Father Aristide decided to run, it was estimated that voter registration doubled in many regions of the country. A champion of poor people and an enemy of the Macoutes, he became an instant favorite to win. I visited Aristide, and he assured me that he would abide by the laws and constitution of Haiti. He insisted, however, that he would win any fair election. He also said that his followers would not accept the results if he lost.

At one political rally just before the election, seven people were killed and fifty injured by Lafontant's supporters, but election day was generally quiet. Our teams went to as many polling places as possible throughout the country. There were scattered but unconfirmed reports of fraud, but the procedures seemed satisfactory. After the polls closed and while the ballots were being counted, I visited several voting places in the poorest parts of Port-au-Prince. There was no electricity, and the election officials and observers were huddled around tables to work by candlelight. Each ballot was passed around and examined before being placed in the proper stack to be counted. The election officials and Haitian observers we had helped train were determined that everything would be done properly.

Of the votes cast, Aristide won more than two-thirds, with his opponents sharing the rest. The people had brought their champion into office, and it seemed that domination by the army and the Tontons Macoutes was ended.

On inauguration day, February 7, 1991, the crowds were so thick that it was almost impossible to reach the cathedral, where a mass of thanksgiving was to be held. Hundreds of thousands of people had gathered in the streets. Many carried roosters, the symbol of the Aristide campaign, or imitated its crow over and over. It was the most impressive demonstration of joy about democracy I have ever seen.

The new president made an eloquent appeal for peace in his country in his inaugural address. He extended a hand of friendship to the army's commanding officer and called for all Haitians to work together toward a better future. All of us who had participated in the election were greatly relieved and excited that the process had worked. Little did we know during this wonderful occasion that the happy people amassed for the inaugural soon would face a tragic future.

Although deeply religious and dedicated to the well-being of the poorest people of Haiti, who had given him their support, Aristide had little understanding of politics or governing. It was almost impossible for him to compromise on any issue, and he failed in his efforts to reach out to Haitian financial, business, educational, and social leaders to join him in the long-overdue reforms. Not trusting the army, he began to organize his own armed security force. There was little cooperation between the new president and the elected members of the parliament. On occasion, when legislators were slow in passing one of Aristide's reform bills, thousands of his supporters would gather around the assembly building and refuse to leave until the legislation was adopted. The international community, including America, relieved that a successful election had been held, did little to assist in resolving the continuing economic and political problems of Haiti. The Carter Center offered to help, but Aristide never responded.

After only eight months in office, President Aristide was overthrown by his opponents, including a new army commander he had appointed. As of early 1993, Aristide is living in exile. Haiti, already the poorest country in our hemisphere, is sinking even further into disorder and poverty.

President Aristide now comes to the Carter Center often to explain his position and to seek our advice and help. The Organization of American States, the U.S. government, the United Nations, and our own Council of Freely Elected Heads of Government are all attempting to resolve this tragedy in a peaceful way. So far, none of these efforts has been successful.

GUYANA

The election in Guyana in 1992 was our most exciting adventure as observers and required us to use all our previous experience.

No one knows the exact demographic makeup of Guyana, but descendants of indentured servants from India constitute about 50 percent of the population, descendants of African slaves perhaps 40 percent, and the rest are of European descent or descendants from tribes of Native Americans. Although there is some crossover, voting is generally divided along ethnic lines. This intriguing country on the northeastern coast of South America won its independence from Great Britain in 1966, but since then had not held an honest election.

In the summer of 1990, as chairman of the Council of Freely Elected Heads of Government, I was asked by opposition political leaders and by President Hugh Desmond Hoyte to organize an international team to assure that the next national election would be open and fair. On a visit to Guyana, I made a list of reforms that would be necessary for us to assure the integrity of the process. The most important were to have an updated voter list, a trusted and balanced election commission, and votes counted at the polling places. The previous practice had been to keep all ballots in locked boxes on election night, to carry them later to central counting places, and to count them a day or two later. The entire process was controlled by the ruling party, and there was serious doubt that the ballots counted were the same ones actually cast by voters. This handling of

Inside the elementary school, there were four separate polling sites. The Guyanese people pressed very tightly into the narrow building to get their chance to vote.

It was October 5, 1992—the first opportunity for ethnically divided Guyana to have a free and fair election in nearly thirty years. The Afro-Guyanese minority had ruled the country during that time, but they feared that the Indo-Guyanese majority could win the election and take their jobs and livelihoods away from them. A lot depended on the outcome of the election, and combined with the morning heat and the pressure of compressed lines, the atmosphere in the school became almost explosive.

The people in the precinct were mostly Africans, but opposition parties were showing some signs of strength. The prime minister, who had a reputation as a tough radical, arrived in the courtyard, and hundreds of people began milling around him, complaining that the registration lists omitted their names and the process was rigged against them. I had heard a few such complaints earlier, but nothing that suggested this was a serious problem. The mob around him now demanded, with increasing intensity, that he put a stop to the fraud.

Suddenly a woman ran out of one of the polling sites, crying that she had been forced by a polling official to vote for one of the opposition parties. The prime minister then led the angry mob into the polling site to intimidate the polling official and try to force her to leave. I ran from the top floor of the school to a room on the first floor where the prime minister and the mob were. I tried to calm everyone and to help the election official—a middle-aged woman—escape the crowd.

There were some tense moments when I feared the woman

would be hurt and the mob would wreck the polling site. But I was able to persuade the prime minister and the crowd to leave. I stayed with the election official until others from our delegation arrived to be with her during the rest of the day.

Elections in ethnically divided societies such as Guyana's are both exciting and dangerous. Mutual suspicions can exaggerate an administrative problem—such as a flawed registration list or a hysterical accusation—until it is assumed that the entire election is corrupt. The presence of international observers in Guyana made the difference between a free election and an ethnic conflict.

ROBERT PASTOR
director, Latin American and
Caribbean Program, the Carter Center

ballots had been the most hotly debated election issue for almost thirty years.

That visit began a long and troubled two years in Guyana, during which the reforms were implemented by laws and constitutional amendments. It took more than eighteen months to develop a voter list acceptable to all political parties. The election was finally scheduled for October 5, 1992. Our observers were to be joined by a few others representing the Commonwealth Organization, but no additional teams were approved by the ruling party.

As always, our team members dispersed on election eve to all regions of the country to observe voting and to report any discrepancies. At the end of the day they were to go back to about 10 percent of the polling places, scientifically selected to be representative of the nationwide vote, to witness and quickly report the vote count. This quick count would have an error margin of less than 3 percent.

As far as the election process was concerned, there were some problems, but no pattern of fraud. I observed my assigned sites in Georgetown, the capital city, early in the day, and found no serious violations. Then I flew up the coast toward the Venezuela border and visited some sites in a jungle area inhabited by Arawak Indians. Everything there was also going well, but as we stepped from our plane on our return to Georgetown, we were surrounded by security agents and observers who said that the election could not be completed. They urged me to go immediately to the U.S. embassy, the only safe place in the city. An uncontrollable mob, perhaps involving the government's supporters, had stormed the election center, pelted it with rocks, and broken all the windows, and the police did not intervene. This was the building where all master voter lists were kept, where the computer system and central radio communications were located, and where all election returns would have to be collected and tabulated.

Instead of the U.S. embassy, I went to our hotel long enough to call the president, who assured me that the police were in control and that the election would go forward. By radio from the site, however, I was informed that the few police present were not attempting to subdue the angry crowd. Instead, violence spread to various parts of the city. (The government newspaper later reported that at least three people were killed, about twenty injured, and one hundred ninety arrested. The nun in charge of the Catholic hospital told me the number of casualties was higher.)

The polls closed at 6:00 P.M., and the slow process of counting the votes began. I was in a quandary but decided that our observers should continue their work wherever it was safe, and that I would go to my quick count site, where everything was quiet. The police commissioner assured me by cellular phone that he had adequate police at the election center to protect the workers, but I was soon informed that the center was still under attack. All the computer and radio operators had abandoned the building and gone to a hotel, taking the master computers with them. They announced that they would receive election returns there, but the hotel manager sent me word that he would forbid this unless "a battalion of troops is sent to protect us against the mobs trying to stop the vote count."

For the second time, it seemed that the election was over. I decided to go to the election center with my small security detail in order to convince the authorities to protect the site and then to induce the workers to return. It was time for the vote tabulations to come in, and no one was there to receive them. When I arrived at a back entrance, there was only one police officer (an unarmed woman) at the center, and several hundred irate citizens were in front of the building. Every window was broken, and glass and other debris were everywhere. I went upstairs to the computer room, which was enclosed and air-conditioned, and called the president again. I told him I was in the unprotected building, and that there was no way to complete the election unless the workers could return. Within ten minutes, the police commissioner arrived, accompanied by about thirty-five police officers, some of whom had side arms. After a few hours, the crowd dispersed.

With the police cordon established, I convinced the election workers to return with their computers and to tabulate the incoming election results. By 1:00 A.M., our quick count showed that the ruling party would lose by a margin of about 14 percent.

Early the next morning, I went to see the two presidential candidates and shared with them our estimate of the results. Both of them agreed to keep this information confidential and to accept the final decision of the voters. During that day, as official returns very slowly became known, I worked with election officials and leaders of the two major parties to insure that everything was done to have a peaceful transition of political authority. Within three days, the new president, Cheddi Jagan, took office.

We left Guyana grateful for this move toward democracy and determined that the Carter Center would stay in close touch with the new government and do everything possible to help the nation's people benefit from their new commitment to freedom and fair play. We were determined not to see the mistakes of Haiti repeated in Guyana.

From Haiti's example, we learned that leaders of new and fragile democracies need continuing advice and support. This and other recent first-time elections also underline the wisdom behind the various democratic institutions crafted by our own Founding Fathers—keeping the people in power depends upon a whole system of governmental checks and balances. We who would champion the cause of democracy around the world cannot assume that our work is done simply because an election has been held.

10

OUR CITIES AT WAR

Seeking Peace in America

In March 1991, an African-American named Rodney King was beaten severely by four white Los Angeles police officers. A bystander managed to videotape the beating, and this tape was shown repeatedly on television. People across the country were shocked by the undeniable brutality of the violence, which seemed to be racially motivated. When a jury with no African-Americans on it, in an affluent suburban neighborhood, decided in April 1992 that the officers were innocent of using excessive force, riots broke out. In the South Central section of Los Angeles, crowds rioted for three days. Sixty people lost their lives; four thousand were injured; nearly twelve thousand people were arrested; and property damage was estimated at nearly $1 billion. Many people believe that the Los Angeles violence was but a single, volcanic instance of an even more serious crisis brewing in our cities.

By the year 2000, nearly five times as many people will live in the world's cities than at the beginning of this century. That equals over half the global population. Cities are often the cultural, educational, and governmental centers of a nation. Urban areas in the United States are the primary source of our ethnic diversity and vitality. But cities also focus and intensify many less-desirable aspects of our society, including homelessness, drug trade, poverty, disease, crime, and sexual and racial violence.

A nation's culture is expressed in how its people dress, worship, dance, and sing; in the foods they eat and the languages they speak; in their values, beliefs, family relationships and histories, and special interests or talents. *Pluralism* is a word that people often use to describe American culture. Pluralism means that there are groups with different cultures who live together in a single community or nation. In our pluralistic culture, the Constitution and its amendments guarantee each of us—no matter what our culture—equal legal rights to life, liberty, and the pursuit of happiness.

The fact is that the legacy of slavery, followed by decades of legal discrimination against women and families of former slaves and other minority groups, has left a nation where these advantages are *not* distributed equally. Although our laws no longer condone outright racial discrimination, when we look at which groups of people are unemployed, which lack adequate education, and which are more prone to homelessness or disease, the contradictions in how people of different races and cultures are still treated in this country become clear. Certainly many wealthy and influential leaders are Hispanic, Asian, or African-American, and many poor people are white. But the heaviest burden of poverty clearly falls on minority groups. And urban communities often most vividly demonstrate this separation between wealthy and poor Americans.

As we've discussed in earlier chapters, when people lack lives of good quality and feel they do not have full representation in their government, they are less likely to be at peace. The Los Angeles riots resulted when thousands of people were convinced that Rodney King had not received the same consideration under the law that a white man would have received.

Months before the Los Angeles riots, we at the Carter Center had begun to focus on the city of Atlanta and its problems. Dr. James T. Laney, the president of Emory University, and I had been talking about how some of the ideas the Carter Center applies in its programs overseas might be useful in helping families here at home. We named this project as simply as we could—the Atlanta Project (TAP)—and began to analyze the problems.

Atlanta is in many respects a great place to live. Recently, *Fortune* magazine said that it was a better place to do business than any other city in America. Atlanta also won the competition to hold the 1996 Olympics. The people of Atlanta can be proud, but serious problems still remain. And I think the very greatness of our city's culture is that we can recognize and begin to treat these troubles.

In Atlanta, which is typical of many other U.S. cities, the drug culture is rampant. Crime is increasing, the jails are overloaded, the school dropout rate is high, and babies have a high mortality rate. Atlanta is a rich city, but the disparity between rich and poor is so great that we have, in effect, two cities. Many Atlantans wake up in the morning and do not know where their next meal is coming from. They don't have jobs, or access to doctors when their children get sick. If they get into trouble, they don't always expect the police to treat them with respect. This sense of hopelessness is shared by an ever-growing number of Americans—including many American leaders, who have tried so many solutions only to see them fail.

How can we tackle the problems of an entire city? I believe it can be done, and that the way to do it is to reach out to each and every person, individual by individual, creating partnerships between rich and poor, young and old, black and white, government and the private sector, educators and students, law enforcement officers and citizens, health care workers and patients. In Atlanta, we're trying to do this—and if we succeed, our project can become a model for other cities around the country.

We have used two criteria to determine which areas of Atlanta are most in need. One is the percentage of families with only one parent (almost always the mother). The other is the percentage of school-age mothers, age sixteen and under. When we identified these areas, we found that we would be dealing with a region where about five hundred thousand people lived. We divided the region into twenty districts surrounding high schools; we call these districts cluster communities. Each cluster has a full-time coordinator, required to be a resident of the community. They help to insure that needy people are the ones who have the power to control programs that are supposed to help them help themselves. A group of highly qualified specialists works with task forces of residents in each community in the fields of health care, education, jobs, safe streets, housing, and community development. Also, a large bank or corporation has formed a close partnership with each cluster community, to help clusters reach their goals. Business leaders realize that creating better communities is a good investment for them and all of Atlanta's citizens. A special effort is being made to forge the same kinds of close ties between the major universities and our targeted communities.

COMMUNITY DEVELOPMENT

Recently I visited seven families who were living in tiny tarpaper shacks in a vacant kudzu field just a hundred yards away from the Carter Center. We might assume on sight that these homeless people were lazy and frightening. But the truth is that they were all looking for jobs. One family had orange crates filled with books in their shack. Another man was a carpenter, who had helped the others build their temporary homes. They told me that one man had been arrested for "urinating in public," although he was in bushes more than fifty feet from a public street. This is an offense that is punishable by up to seventeen days in the local jail. They believe the community encourages the police to arrest them rather than provide them with toilets. They consider this a form of harassment, designed to get them to move out of so-called respectable neighborhoods. What they deserve is a decent place to live.

Just three blocks north of the Carter Center is an organization called the Open Door. There are many groups like this one, both in Atlanta and in other communities across the country. Thirty formerly homeless people, most of whom are recovering alcoholics and drug abusers, now live together. With the help of a dedicated religious couple and other volunteers, they prepare and serve ten thousand meals a month to other homeless people. They are justly proud of what they have been doing to help their fellow human beings—they have done much more than many of us. This is what community development can accomplish; it can empower people in need to help one another, and it can encourage the rest of us to join in, not saying, "I am better than you," but asking, "What can we do together to make this a really great city?"

We've spent a lot of time in the cluster communities with the people who live there, learning about their needs and priorities. TAP is not a charity organization. After the residents determine their own objectives, we will marshal all the help possible, working with them, their coordinators, and their corporate partners, to help reach their goals. We are identifying all the services already available—from government programs, nonprofit organizations, religious congregations, and many individual volunteers. The general goal is to build on successful ideas to form friendly cooperation among all citizens of our community. A number of specific projects will be possible. Here are a few examples:

- Lawyers and senior-year law students will provide free legal services. Others will serve as voluntary probation workers, helping juvenile delinquents, already convicted of a serious crime, to have a friend, find a job, and receive encouragement with schoolwork.
- Artists, musicians, and dancers will share their talents with interested students, either during or after regular school hours.

- Doctors, medical students, and nurses will strengthen the services of health clinics and insure that all young children are immunized against preventable diseases.
- Volunteers will work together to build new homes, repair those that are dilapidated, or just be on call to help an elderly homeowner fix a leaky faucet or a sticky window, or replace a rotten step.
- Bankers will insure that service in poor neighborhoods is equal to that given their wealthier customers.

HEALTH CARE

At the beginning of the Atlanta Project, Rosalynn and I visited a public hospital to see what might be done about infant mortality. The number of babies that die each year in the state of Georgia is very high. At Grady Hospital, there was a little baby named Pumpkin who had been born prematurely at five months, weighing only one pound two ounces. Her mother was addicted to crack and so obese that she had not even realized that she was pregnant until the baby was born in the woman's bathroom. Luckily, Pumpkin has survived, but bringing her up to a normal weight has cost the taxpayers three hundred thousand dollars. If Pumpkin's mother had been given adequate prenatal care—as well as help for her addiction—this might have been prevented. Thirty percent of mothers who go to Grady Hospital to give birth have not had adequate prenatal care—and one out of six babies born here is addicted to crack cocaine. This problem exists in many urban communities, all over America.

Our goal is to encourage Atlanta doctors to volunteer a few hours each week. Every pregnant woman should receive prenatal care. All babies born in the city should be fully inoculated against diseases before they are two years old. Every child who lives in a housing project should be guaranteed good health care, as should those who live in affluent areas.

The Atlanta Project is developing programs by which we can measure these and other concrete goals. For example, about fifty-four thousand children under the age of five live within the boundaries of the Atlanta Project, and one half of them have not been properly immunized against preventable childhood diseases such as measles and whooping cough. Yet immunization is one of the most cost-effective means of health care. One dollar spent on immunization saves ten dollars that would have to be spent later treating these diseases.

In the spring of 1993, the Atlanta Project marshaled thousands of volunteers throughout its neighborhoods to spread that message. These volunteers helped teach their neighbors about the importance and benefits of proper immunization and even drove them to sites where their children were immunized. This is one step in a long-term commitment to the health of our children and to increased awareness among their parents.

EDUCATION

In an Atlanta middle school not long ago, the students were asking me very hard questions—stimulating questions that I hadn't heard anywhere else. One sixth grader asked, "President Carter, why do some old people lose their Social Security?" Being familiar with the law, I assured her that this did not happen unless the person began to earn a lot more money. She replied, "Well, my grandfather doesn't earn any money. He lives under a bridge in west Atlanta, and they took his away because he doesn't have a mailing address." This is the kind of question I wouldn't get in my own grandchildren's school. (Later, I discussed this case with the regional Social Security administrator, who promised to investigate and resolve the problem. Although I was glad to help, it shouldn't be necessary for a former president to intervene.)

Afterward, I asked their principal what the main problems were in the school. She said that many of the boys believed that their future success, their status in life, was dependent on their owning a semiautomatic weapon. When I asked her about the girls, she told me that getting pregnant was probably their biggest problem—and especially among sixth graders, who are usually only twelve years old. She said this was true because these very young girls have trouble defending themselves and are more attractive to older men because they are less likely to have AIDS than older girls.

The problems in the lives of these young people are very complicated and have no simple solutions. Troubled children must be identified and helped on an individual basis. Every teacher in every classroom needs to have one or more aides so that students can receive more individual attention. Moreover, school resources need to be improved—this means better books and teaching materials, but also improved playgrounds, athletic equipment, and facilities for other extracurricular activities. Major corporations and banks that are participating in the Atlanta Project soon realize that any investment in our schools will pay off down the road in more stable and better-trained employees.

Most of the youth in my community feel as if society is their greatest enemy. Their actual enemy is society's misperception of what really goes on with gang wars, drug deals, armed robberies, and high school dropouts. But wrong attitudes can block good communication. In tense situations, people tend to overexaggerate, turning them into something unbearable. Many people are just too stubborn to listen to what others have to say. Somehow, there must be more talking, sharing, and listening, so that emotions can be voiced.

Violence has become a greater factor in my community than communication. Young adults are robbed and often killed over petty items such as shoes and jackets. Many individuals in my community have an excessive amount of aggression. The aggression comes from a mental agitation that affects their self-confidence —and this type of confusion plays a large role in violent alterca-

CRIME

As in many other places across the country, statistics on crime in the Atlanta area are discouraging. In a recent five-year period, crimes in our juvenile court involving weapons have increased 73 percent, robberies 240 percent, violent crimes 300 percent, and drug-related crimes 1,700 percent. The situation has been growing worse, not better.

Law enforcement officials agree that just building more jails will not solve our crime problems. An emphasis on stricter punishments will not solve them. It costs about $35,000 a year to keep an inmate in prison—more than to attend Harvard University. A small portion of this would pay rich dividends,

tions. Many violent reactions between individuals occur without any thought on the part of either party.

Even though violence and communication are problems to solve within themselves, without a good education, these young people will lead lives that are fruitless anyway. Students need to be given more motivation to learn. The schools are not entirely to blame. Innumerable students have reached the short-attention-span era, where nothing is interesting for more than ten minutes. Talking more, learning to solve problems without violence, and gaining a desire to stay in school and do well there will all help.

We are talking about the lives of a future generation, lives with a great many problems right now. No one person or organization can do it alone, but a collaboration between all of us can make a great difference.

HERCULES CROOM
a high school student participating
in the Atlanta Project

properly spent to provide better education, job opportunities, and safer neighborhoods. Better connections between individuals—a more closely knit society—can help solve the crime problem. In my opinion, we can begin by focusing on the needs of sixth graders, perhaps even of younger children.

We need to identify kids when they first begin missing classes and determine how they can be helped and motivated. I firmly believe that a little caring will make a world of difference. If requested by the teacher, an adult mentor could get to know a student and say, "OK, let me meet you and your family. I will be glad to help you with your classwork." A juvenile delinquent,

The Facts: Children, Adolescents, and Firearms

- An estimated two hundred million firearms exist in the United States. In one out of every four homes, there is a handgun.
- Handguns account for the majority of firearm deaths and injuries.
- As of 1988, one out of six pediatricians reported that he or she had treated a child for a gun-related injury.
- No other country in the world has as many deaths caused by firearms in peacetime. Death by firearms is an American epidemic.
- Studies show a gun in the home is more likely to kill a family member or friend than to be used to kill an intruder: forty-three times more likely in one study.
- In the last twenty years, firearm deaths among teenagers has risen 75 percent.
- Handguns were used in 73 percent of teenage homicides due to firearms and 70 percent of teenage suicides due to firearms.
- A common misperception is that teen homicides are largely related to crime, gang activity, or premeditated assault. In fact, the majority of shootings are committed by friends or relatives, usually because of an argument later seen as trivial, according to the Centers for Disease Control.
- Comparing international data from five to six years ago, firearm homicides in U.S. males aged fifteen to twenty-four totaled three thousand one hundred eighty-seven. Firearm homicides in males from seven other developed countries in the same age group totaled seventy-two—only 2 percent of the U.S. figure.
- More male teens are killed by guns than by all natural causes of death (heart disease, cancer, etc.).
- An African-American male between the ages of fifteen and twenty-

four is eleven times more likely to be murdered with a gun than his Caucasian counterpart.

- Texas, California, and New York lead in firearm homicides among Caucasian males aged fifteen to twenty-four, while Michigan, Washington, D.C., and California have the highest firearm homicides among African-American males in the same age group.
- Media portrayals and societal factors influence dangerous gun-use patterns by children, adolescents, and adults.
- No product safety regulations currently exist for handguns or ammunition.

Source: The American Academy of Pediatrics. The American Academy of Pediatrics supports legislative and regulatory measures, including the banning of specific weapon categories, to reduce children's accessibility to firearms. Eliminating handguns from the environment of children and adolescents is the surest way to reduce the trauma that the use of these weapons inflicts on children and adolescents.

coming out of the court system either on probation or having finished a detention sentence, could accept counseling and assistance from someone skilled in the law.

One of the most promising ideas is the formation of strong "safe streets" committees among parents in troubled neighborhoods. They could work with police officers on a better system of reporting drug pushers and other criminals without fear of being abused themselves when the criminal is released. Government housing officials and law enforcement officers are beginning to join in removing nonqualified residents from public housing, often the center of the drug trade. In every project, local residents are taking the initiative, with maximum support from existing agencies.

HOUSING

There are about twelve thousand homeless people in Atlanta. Many other families live in substandard housing; some live in government housing that is neither safe nor decent. An increasing number of working families now cannot find affordable, adequate dwellings because federal construction funds for low-income housing have been cut by 92 percent since 1980. Others have homes that are deteriorating around them because they cannot get insurance coverage or bank loans for necessary repairs. More than a thousand people cannot find even temporary shelter at night, and this figure includes many children.

We are approaching the housing problem and the problems of temporary care for homeless people on many different levels. My experience at Habitat for Humanity has taught me that religious congregations are a great resource for building houses. If twenty or thirty people band together to build or renovate a home, working side by side with the people who will live in the home, both they and the new homeowners will benefit. This kind of volunteer work can be exciting, challenging, and exhilarating.

Several of America's large private foundations regularly send delegations from cities around the country to describe projects that have been successful in their own communities. From these reports, our cluster community residents learn how the same kind of effort might work for them. What we as a people need, and what I think we will have in the Atlanta Project, is a united effort where all of us, no matter how diverse our backgrounds, our hopes, our fears, our aspirations, or our concerns, can join together. *There is a desperate need all across the country for a sense of community.* In Atlanta, we already have businesses; banks; federal, state, and local government officials; private organizations such as the United Way; and many thousands of volunteers working together. My hope is that a large number of mothers who have been successful in raising a child will offer to help a teenage girl through her pregnancy. Many high school graduates—or older high school students—could become mentors for sixth-grade truants. Almost every business could provide some kind of resource, training, or employment for out-of-work but employable adults.

Not long ago, I went to London and spoke about the Atlanta Project to a distinguished audience, including the Prince of Wales and four former prime ministers of Great Britain. I discovered that these same problems we have been talking about are as common to British cities as they are to all of urban America. If America is to continue to be a world leader into the twenty-first century, we must hold to our new visions, new solutions, and new successes and share them as best we can. Imagine what a partnership like the Atlanta Project could accomplish in your own city or neighborhood.

11

THE STATUS
OF YOUNG PEOPLE

Children's Rights around the World

I am sure you have often heard adults complain, "Things were different when I was a teenager" or "Children are growing up faster than ever before." Familiar as these phrases may be, they are undoubtedly true. The pressures on young people today are quite different from those faced by earlier generations of Americans. When I was growing up in Plains, Georgia, I never knew anyone who was divorced. The only single-parent families were those in which the husband or wife had died. All across the community, family units were solid, almost unshakable. Marriage vows were taken as binding for life, even if a few spouses found it impossible to get along with each other and decided to live separately. Almost all of us boys used guns for hunting, but we certainly would never have considered taking a weapon to school. We were tempted to drink alcohol and to smoke, but other drugs were nowhere to be found, and the disease of AIDS did not exist. The daily behavioral choices that we made were less fraught with danger and disease than those you face today.

As teenagers, most of you probably do not consider yourselves children anymore. You have moved into the world of adult privileges and responsibilities and have a lot more control over your own time. You have more freedom to make choices about your life—what classes you will take; whether you will go to college and, if so, where; what extracurricular activities you wish to pursue. Yet legally, until you become eighteen, you are still a child, and your parents are responsible for you. In this country, if a child or adolescent is orphaned, it is the state's responsibility to serve in place of the parents to provide for that child's basic needs. Children and adolescents cannot legally drink, vote, or live alone. It is against the law for children to conduct certain business transactions, and it is even illegal for children to see some movies. These prohibitions may seem strange or irrelevant to you, considering the array of serious choices you make every day about your activities and well-being.

What is our society doing to help young people make wise choices? Help for children comes from many different sources, including the family, local governments, religious organizations, private volunteers, and schools. Most people feel that in recent years the issues that affect children—education, housing, health care, drugs, crime, teen pregnancy, and family support—have not had a high enough priority.

We in America need to do more. Worldwide, interest in the

welfare of children is at an all-time high. In the fall of 1990, an assembly of world leaders, called the World Summit for Children, was held at the United Nations in New York. Seventy-one presidents and prime ministers attended—an unprecedented number. Together with representatives of eighty-six other nations, they agreed upon a set of standards for the health and well-being of the world's children. These standards include reducing the infant death rate by one-third; providing safe water for all families; cutting the rate of adult illiteracy in half; reducing unwanted pregnancies; fostering better nutrition; immunizing 90 percent of all children before the age of two years; protecting children in especially difficult circumstances, such as war; and universally recognizing the special health and nutritional needs of females.

One hundred thirty-four countries are developing or implementing specific national plans to accomplish these goals, and one hundred twenty-five countries have ratified an agreement known as the Convention on the Rights of the Child. The United States is one of the few countries and the only Western democracy that has not yet signed the convention. Some of our government leaders have claimed that the convention might change the legal relationship between children and their parents. They also say that it has different definitions of human rights than those in the U.S. Constitution. For instance, the convention condemns the death penalty as a punishment for minors, a provision that is in conflict with some state laws. Although our national laws *do* secure most of the basic rights for American children regardless of whether or not the convention is signed, it is still important for the United States to support this international agreement. Our influence is so strong that if we do not sign, we may indirectly encourage other nations to ignore the important provisions they have adopted.

Obviously, the United States provides much more for children than many other countries do. We offer free education through high school for all; the quality and breadth of our university system is unequaled on earth; and basic freedoms are guaranteed by our Constitution. Ours is the best of nations, but there is little doubt that our government can do better in addressing the needs of children.

UNICEF has calculated that the percentage of children in the United States living in poverty increased from 14 percent in the 1960s to 22 percent in the 1980s. Homelessness has risen. Our infant mortality rate, although low by some standards, is among the highest of all industrialized nations. Our nation ranks thirty-second in the world in meeting the needs of our minority children and seventeenth in services for all children. And while great progress has been made around the world in immunizing children against five preventable diseases—measles, diphtheria, whooping cough, tetanus, and polio—major health crises among children are still possible in the United States. For example, over twenty-seven thousand cases of measles were reported in this country in 1990. Although health practitioners have now succeeded in lowering this high rate, we should remember that ten years earlier the disease had almost disappeared here.

Government leaders explain that many problems exist because there is not money to pay for solutions. They would like to provide job training and day-care services or to build more low-income housing, better schools, drug rehabilitation centers, libraries, and recreation facilities—but with our huge federal deficit, many leaders feel that America can't afford it. We can't

A single horrifying event triggered a big change in the way I thought about my relationship to life itself. One afternoon in April 1989, I walked out of a baseball stadium and saw my son, Albert, then six years old, get hit by a car, fly thirty feet through the air, and scrape along the pavement another twenty feet until he came to rest in a gutter. I ran to his side and held him and called his name, but he was motionless, limp and still, without breath or pulse. His eyes were open with the nothingness stare of death, and we prayed, the two of us, there in the gutter, with only my voice. Slowly, painfully, he fought through his shock and fear and latched on to the words as a beacon to find his way back to the street, where others now gathered, including two off-duty nurses, who, thank God, knew enough about the medical realities to keep him alive in spite of his massive injuries inside and out. When the ambulance finally arrived, the technicians took a long time trying to stabilize his vital signs enough to leave the scene safely; finally they raced to the emergency room and the next phase of what became an epic struggle by dozens of skilled men and women to hang on to a dear and precious life.

For the next month, my wife, Tipper, and I stayed in the hospi-

afford *not* to address these problems. The breakup of the Soviet Union and the ending of the cold war have given us an unprecedented opportunity to rethink our $300 billion defense budget. Each year, this money equals about $1,200 for every American adult and child. Among domestic programs, there are numerous opportunities to change priorities. Many expensive government services, such as health care, go to wealthy citizens

tal with our son. For many more months, our lives were completely consumed with the struggle to restore his body and spirit. And for me something changed in a fundamental way. I began to realize how fragile life is, and I felt a new sense of urgency about those things I value most, including my family and the world we live in.

This life change has caused me to be increasingly impatient with the complacent and lazy assumption that we can always muddle through. Such thinking has allowed many kinds of difficult problems to breed and grow, particularly the destruction of the global environment. We have been guilty of using the natural resources that sustain us without concern for preserving or protecting the environment for future generations. We have ignored the increasing threat we pose to the environment, and because of that, now no one can afford to assume that the world will somehow solve its problems.

Now, we must all become partners in a bold effort to change our civilization, and to work to protect and restore the world around us.

AL GORE
vice president of the United States

who could afford to pay the bills themselves. Well-balanced tax increases could also help provide needed funds. Our country must regain the opportunity to become a world leader for children, both by speaking out on their behalf in the international arena and by urging more support for children's issues at home. We cannot let the next generation down.

Whether or not you are legally an adult, even if you are too young to vote, you can still help the country find solutions to the long-term, complex problems that affect the quality of family and community life. To change our priorities as a society, we must all use our private influence to put pressure on the political system.

I know from my own experience in running for office how much candidates depend on young people, not only to run errands, hand out pamphlets, and answer the telephones, but for ideas on what our government should do. In the 1960s, I saw my own sons and their friends change our nation's policies by working against the Vietnam War, supporting civil rights, and organizing the first Earth Day to protect the environment. When I ran for governor in 1970, my strongest supporter in northeast Georgia was a high school student named Scott Douglass, who was only fifteen years old. He rode his bike through the streets and along country roads, nailing up posters for me. I listened closely to his views. Later, when I ran for president, Scott was a college student and still had an intense interest in public affairs. He helped me again, driving me around on some of my campaign trips and organizing other young people to work in the campaign. He also went to Washington to work in the federal government when I moved to the White House.

Political leaders are eager to have both support and advice from young people like Scott. You really can make a difference in this way, and perhaps at the same time prepare yourself for a political career of your own.

12

WHAT YOU CAN DO

A Vision for the Future

By now, this book may have raised more questions for you than it has answered. Where can you go to find out more?

First, the library in your school or neighborhood is an excellent resource. Read as much as you can about what is going on around the globe. Watch the news and listen to the radio. If you hear the name of an unfamiliar place or country, don't just let it go—look it up, and you'll be connecting yourself a little bit more to the world around you.

Second, an excellent way to further the cause of peace is to communicate your concerns to others. Teachers, family members, friends, and organizations in your community and state have a lot to learn from young people. Around the table at mealtimes in the White House, my own children helped me with ideas about many major issues, including education. I learned a lot about the need for financial assistance for poor families trying to support students in college from my youngest son and his classmates at George Washington University. An even more valuable contribution came from our daughter, Amy, who gave us daily reports about the public school system in Washington. We used this kind of personal information as we shaped the nation's new Department of Education. I still have "town meetings" in high schools and on college campuses several times a year to stay aware of how young Americans feel about major domestic and foreign issues. If you feel strongly about communicating with a person you cannot easily meet, like a government leader or a company director, write him or her a letter. By sharing your point of view, you'll be encouraging other people to help you achieve your goals.

Third, take some time to reflect on what you have learned. The issues covered in this book are extremely complex. Many of them are accompanied by powerful images of suffering that may be disturbing to you. As you learn even more about the causes and the conflicts that have moved you, you may discover that simple answers are more elusive than ever. Consider keeping a journal: Record in it your discoveries and ideas about current events; your reactions to conflict in your own life; your hopes and plans for the future. A private diary can be an excellent companion when you are tackling problems that are fundamental to our very survival. Each day while president, I dictated my thoughts on interesting events that would not be reported in the public records. When a tape was full, my secretary would type what I had dictated. After leaving the White House, I was surprised to find six thousand pages of private notes. Someday they will make an interesting addition to the more formal history of the presidency. Much of the material for this book came from my own trip logs and notes that I have kept over the years.

One big question you may have is *Why me?* Why do I need to know about the people at war in Africa or Asia, so far away, living in cultures so different from my own? As we have discussed, the world is getting smaller in a very real sense. What we do in this country impacts people in other nations—and vice versa. You may have had a friend or relative who fought in the Persian Gulf War. You may know someone who was injured in the Los Angeles riots—or someone who was killed by violence in your own neighborhood. As an active American citizen, you can help shape your own life, your community, your city, and even the policies of your national government.

Soon you will cast your first vote. With that ballot, you will help to choose the leaders of the most powerful country in the world. Your decision will have an impact on millions of lives and on the fate of the environment as well. Remember, too, that many local leaders are elected, as well as your state government representatives. Too few Americans pay attention to these smaller, less-glamorous races, yet the men and women who fill these offices may have the greatest impact on our daily lives. They regulate housing, the police force, municipal garbage and recycling programs, public transportation systems, juvenile courts, and schools, among many other things. Your vote should be an educated one. Elections are the key to unlocking all of what is best about democracy and individual freedoms.

Besides voting, there is a lot that citizens can do to influence the programs of the people elected to office. One young student

I grew up in the same town in Georgia as Jimmy Carter, and he had a great influence over my entire family. Beginning when I was very young, my father sharecropped with him. When Mr. Carter left farming to get involved in politics, my father continued to harvest the crops on his farm.

In the 1960s, my sister was one of the first ten black children to attend the all-white Plains High School as part of an experimental integration program. There was racial violence at the school, but a man named Jimmy Carter continued to work for justice and peace for all children, regardless of race, creed, or color. By the time I attended Plains High School in the 1970s, it was fully integrated.

When I was in my early teens, I baby-sat for the Carters' youngest child, Amy. I felt like part of the family. After I graduated from high school, many companies in my area had hiring freezes. I didn't know which way to turn for a career. I started working for a day-care center until my parents got a call from the Carters asking if any of us children wanted to work on the Carter

eventually convinced the major American fast-food chains to alter packaging habits that were damaging the environment. A young girl's letter to a Soviet leader, expressing her fears about nuclear war, helped inspire him to conduct disarmament talks. A twelve-year-old in New Jersey petitioned state officials and testified before the legislature to get a shocking series of racist television commercials pulled off the air. Just the names of Prime Minister Begin's grandchildren reminded him to persevere in the Camp David negotiations. Young people can have an effect.

campaign in Plains. I immediately said yes, and starting that job was the best thing that ever happened to me, leading eventually to a job in the White House.

While working on that first campaign, I realized how much I wanted to make a difference with my life and in my community. Being involved in the political process made me understand that voting was one of the best ways to do it, so I registered for the first time.

The interest the Carters had in making life better for those who were less fortunate also inspired me to become more involved in my church community as a young adult. Today, I realize there are lots of ways people can make a difference, from feeding the homeless to providing food and clothing to families in need. It doesn't matter where you start or how you choose to help others, but the most important thing is to start somewhere and to stay involved.

BERNSTINE W. HOLLIS
assistant to the financial comptroller,
the Carter Center

As you read this book, I hope one or two of the issues held particular meaning for you. Each of us has unique interests, skills, and talents, and it is when we act from our hearts, with our minds, through our hands that we are most satisfied and effective. Choose one issue that interests you, figure out how much time you want to devote, and get involved. If you like talking, maybe you can work on a teen hot line. If you like to write, perhaps you can create a community news column for your school paper. If you like to be physically active, perhaps you can get involved in a building project for the homeless. If no organized activities in your neighborhood appeal to you, recruit some friends and start a committee of your own!

Here are a few more specific ideas.

CONFLICT

- Ask one of your teachers to set aside part of the classroom for a conflict board. Put up a world map and, with other students, monitor conflicts that are going on around the world. If you can't find enough coverage of the situations that interest you on television or in the papers, write to the Carter Center and let us know.

FOOD, SHELTER, AND HEALTH

- Find out if there are any soup kitchens or homeless shelters in your area. Recruit other volunteers to help you organize a food, clothing, or toy drive. Perhaps an extracurricular group, like a chorus, sports team, or band, could sponsor the event.

- Ask a doctor to help you take a Health Risk Appraisal. Be honest with yourself in the choices you make about smoking, drinking, drugs, and sex. Soon you alone will be responsible for your actions, your health, and your future.

ENVIRONMENT

- Does your family recycle? Do your neighbors? Your parents' offices? Your school? If any of these groups don't, help them start a program.

- At the library, figure out where your gas and electric power come from and where the garbage that is collected from your family goes. If you can, visit the utility and recycling companies and the landfills. Do you agree with the way your community's natural resources are being used? Is unnecessary pollution occurring? Write your local political leaders and tell them what you think.

- Take a look at the empty lots in your neighborhood. With permission from the owners and some volunteer work, they can be cleaned up and divided into family garden plots for flowers or vegetables, or perhaps furnished with some home-made playground equipment.

HUMAN RIGHTS

- Amnesty International and many other human rights organizations welcome young members. Ask your librarian for the address or phone number of the chapters near you.
- If you hear about human rights abuses in this country or far away, write your national congressional representatives and/or the president and ask them to take action.

MEDIATION

- Talk to guidance counselors or teachers about starting a student mediation team in your school. With their help or the help of an outside professional, you can learn how to understand the causes of conflicts and work toward fair and unanimous solutions. Use these new skills at school, at home, and in your neighborhood.

ELECTIONS

- If you are interested in politics, find out how the candidates stand on the issues you care about by calling the local office of the Democratic Party, the Republican Party, or the League of Women Voters. Volunteer for the campaign of someone you trust, and you may be surprised by the responsibilities you are given to handle.

- If there are problems in your school you'd like to address, run for student government or manage someone else's campaign. If the election results are reached fairly, accept them with good grace whether you win or lose.

CITIES

- Become a big brother or sister to an underprivileged child in your neighborhood. If no organized program exists, ask a teacher, guidance counselor, or church leader to help you start one.
- Ask drug enforcement officials or other police officers to visit your class and give you the facts about drugs and gangs in your area. Ask them what steps you can take to protect yourself from drug-related violence.

All of us have to face disappointments, and sometimes what seems like failure. I overcame many challenges in my first election for state senator, even while I made a lot of mistakes. Because of fraud in the election, I had to go through a series of political arguments and several court trials before the victory was declared mine by a narrow margin. Later, when I ran for governor, I lost. But I came back in four years and was elected. In each case, winning or losing, I learned a lot about the people in my state, the important issues, and myself. These experiences made it possible for me to become president.

When my family and I left the White House earlier than we wished, we had to change our careers, but we have found a good new life. Our work at the Carter Center is satisfying and important, and each day we learn something from others or from experience that makes our lives more interesting and adventurous. With the dramatic, often violent, changes occurring at this time in history, it is important for all of us to learn how to best use our talents—not only for ourselves, but for a better and more peaceful world.

You as an individual fill many different roles in life already: student, friend, sibling, daughter or son. Many of you are also athletes, singers, dancers, writers, and artists. Some of you may know the urban skills of the streets; others know more about the ways of rural life. Regardless of what your interests or talents may be, you can also fill a larger role in the world.

To work for better understanding among people, one does not have to be a former president sitting at a fancy conference room table. Peace can be made in the neighborhoods, the living rooms, the playing fields, and the classrooms of our country. No matter how old you are or what your situation in life might be, you still make the personal choices we have talked about in this book and you are still in charge of your own destiny. Together, regardless of age, sex, race, or nationality, we can all work toward a time when the world is no longer suffering from the tragedies of neglect, war, and oppression—but enjoying the glow of caring, freedom, and peace.

About the Author

Jimmy Carter (James Earl Carter, Jr.) was born October 1, 1924, in the small farming town of Plains, Georgia, and grew up in the nearby community of Archery. His father, James Earl Carter, Sr., was a farmer and a businessman; his mother, Lillian Gordy, a registered nurse.

He was educated in the Plains public schools, attended Georgia Southwestern College and the Georgia Institute of Technology, and received a bachelor of science degree from the United States Naval Academy in 1946. He later did graduate work in nuclear physics at Union College. During his naval career, he served with both the Atlantic and Pacific fleets and rose to the rank of lieutenant (senior grade), working under Admiral Hyman Rickover in the development of the nuclear submarine program.

On July 7, 1946, he married Rosalynn Smith. In 1953, he resigned his commission and they returned to Plains. He worked his own farm and continued a small business of his father's, selling fertilizer and farm supplies, while Rosalynn kept the books. Carter's Warehouse grew into a profitable general-purpose seed and farm supply operation.

Soon after his return to Plains, he became chairman of the county school board and the first president of the Georgia Planning Association. In 1962, he was elected to the Georgia Senate. He lost his first gubernatorial campaign in 1966, but in 1970 he succeeded, becoming Georgia's seventy-sixth governor.

On December 12, 1974, he announced his candidacy for president; he won his party's endorsement at the 1976 Democratic National Convention on the first ballot. He was elected on November 2, 1976.

Jimmy Carter served as president from January 20, 1977, to January 20, 1981. Noteworthy foreign policy accomplishments of his administration included the Panama Canal treaties, the Camp David Accords, the treaty of peace between Egypt and Israel, the SALT II treaty with the Soviet Union, and the establishment of diplomatic relations with the People's Republic of China. He championed human rights throughout the world. On the domestic side, the administration's achievements included a comprehensive energy program conducted by a new Department of Energy; major educational programs under a new Department of Education; and major environmental protection legislation, including the Alaska Lands Act.

In 1982, he became University Distinguished Professor at Emory University, in Atlanta, Georgia, and, in partnership with the university, founded the Carter Center.

President Carter has served on the board of directors and is a regular volunteer for Habitat for Humanity, a nonprofit organization that helps build homes for the needy in the United States and in underdeveloped countries. He also teaches Sunday school and is a deacon in the Maranatha Baptist Church, in Plains.

An avid fly-fisherman and woodworker, President Carter has written articles on both subjects for various publications. His other hobbies include jogging, cycling, tennis, and skiing.

Notes

The author would like to thank the following people in particular for adding their voices to *Talking Peace:* John F. Burns, Rosalynn Carter, Hercules Croom, Al Gore, Dr. John Hardman, Bernstine W. Hollis, Jim Johnson, James T. Lester III, Eugene Linden, Robert Pastor, and William Watson. John F. Burns's reporting is copyright © 1992 by The New York Times Company. Reprinted by permission.

President Carter's letter to Prime Minister Begin of August 3, 1978, is reprinted courtesy of the Jimmy Carter Library, Atlanta, Georgia.

"Instances of the Use of United States Armed Forces Abroad" is based on two studies by the Congressional Research Service of the Library of Congress: "Instances of Use of United States Armed Forces Abroad, 1798–1989," edited by Ellen C. Collier (December 4, 1989), and "War Powers Resolution: Presidential Compliance," by Ellen C. Collier (November 9, 1992).

"Armed Conflicts" is based on a synopsis of conflicts accompanying the article "As Ethnic Wars Multiply, U.S. Strives for a Policy," by David Binder with Barbara Crossette, the *New York Times* (February 7, 1993). Copyright © 1993 by The New York Times Company. Reprinted by permission.

Data for The Map of Freedom is used courtesy of Freedom House, New York, New York. Their Comparative Survey of Freedom analyzes factors in each country, such as the degree to which fair and competitive elections occur, individual and group freedoms are guaranteed in practice, and press freedoms exist. In some cases, the categories chosen reflect active citizen opposition rather than political rights granted by a government.

"Primary Forest Remaining in Selected Regions" is based on *State of the World 1991: A Worldwatch Institute Report on Progress Toward a Sustainable Society,* W. W. Norton & Company, New York, New York.

"The Facts: Children, Adolescents, and Firearms" is reprinted courtesy of the American Academy of Pediatrics.

Index

FRANKLIN PIERCE COLLEGE LIBRARY

00076622

DATE DUE

NOV 27 1994 DEC. 7 9 1994		
JUL 2 9 '96		
NOV 2 9 '98		
FEB 1 8 2003		
MAY 07 2007		
MAY 07 2007		

GAYLORD

PRINTED IN U.S.A.